Midland Spirits & Spectres

by Anne Bradford & Barrie Roberts

Quercus

***** back title

****
QuercuS
John Roberts
67 Cliffe Way, Warwick CV34 5JG
Tel/Fax 01926 776363
****

Midland Spirits & Spectres

by Anne Bradford & Barrie Roberts

ISBN 1 898136 16 5

First Published 1998

Preface

Midland Ghosts & Hauntings was published in the Autumn of 1994. It contained 51 stories of strange events from all over the Midlands which Anne and Barrie had collected from responses to their newspaper appeals. Inevitably, we had more stories than we could comfortably handle in one book, and the surplus immediately suggested a sequel. Sales of *Ghosts & Hauntings* certainly suggested that the public would like to see one. None of the stories in this book appeared in the first one and the vast majority have never been published before.

The Authors

ANNE BRADFORD published her first book of ghost stories in July 1992. She is well qualified to collect anecdotes from the Midlands, having lived in Hockley, Ladywood, Edgbaston, The Malverns, West Hagley, Handsworth, Smethwick and Studley, eventually settling in Redditch. Her very first article was published at the age of 8 in the Smethwick Telephone and has dabbled in freelance journalism ever since. She was a mature student at Shenstone Teacher Training College, is married to a Graphic Designer and has three children, all of whom have flown the nest.

BARRIE ROBERTS is a former criminal lawyer who specialised in the analysis of evidence. He is now a consultant on the paranormal, writer and lecturer. For nearly ten years he has taught a unique evening course on Ghosts and Unsolved Mysteries for the City of Birmingham and has recently finished teaching a two year course on the Assassination of John Kennedy. He is the author of *Sherlock Holmes and the Railway Maniac, Sherlock Holmes and the Devil's Grail, Sherlock Holmes and the Man from Hell, Sherlock Holmes and the Royal Flush as well as a contemporary thriller - The Victory Snapshot.* Barrie is one of the authors of the predecessor to this book, *Midland Ghosts & Hauntings,* and he has recently written *Midland Murders & Mysteries* for Quercus.

Contents

"Do you believe in Ghosts?"

When we wrote *Midland Ghosts & Hauntings* we explained that in selecting the stories we had been forced to leave out many simple, undramatic accounts of paranormal experiences, and we had to make the same choices in this sequel. However, by their very ordinariness and abundance, these stories seem the best proof that ghosts have some kind of reality. The fact that the most ordinary people experience ghostly manifestations everyday, in the most commonplace circumstances, stresses the need to examine and test these phenomena until we understand how they operate.

Midland Ghosts etc started with a chapter, 'There are no such things as Ghosts', quite simply because this is the first thing many people say to any mention of the subject. There is no point in reprinting that chapter, but here are its main points mixed with some further thoughts.

The enormous, continuing flood of accounts of inexplicable events from so many people and so many places makes it useless to say that there is nothing that needs explaining. Nor is it convincing to say that all witnesses are deluded or dishonest, or that all their experiences can be explained by things which we call natural, such as creaking floorboards. To try to do this suggests that we know everything there is to be known about all phenomena and that there is nothing we cannot now explain. No scientist could assert this. We have to accept, at the very least, that most or many of the witnesses are offering a true account of their experiences, whatever the explanation for them may be. Not the least interesting fact is that so many of the experiences seem to be similar or comparable, suggesting that (whatever their nature) they have some sort of objective reality.

The previous book was called *Ghosts & Hauntings* - this is *Spirits & Spectres.* They had to have titles which people would recognise, but these convenient labels get in the way of clear thinking because they lump together all sorts of things. We have phantom cats, misty Cavaliers, visions of ancient battles, objects flying around rooms, monks in black habits that float through walls, and walking, talking images of people who died many years ago. Very many other strange things are reported, including smells of tobacco and flowers, changes of temperature and intelligible messages. There is no reason at all to think that these things have the same origins or work in the same way; they might prove to be just as different, and in another way as related, as electricity and gravity, or sound and light. To deal with one popular assumption, there is no evidence that all or any of these strange events have the remotest connection with the spirits of the dead or with witchcraft.

We do not know how to explain these strange events which are experienced by thousands of people, and to place them all under the same heading is confusing. At the same time, it does seem possible to place many of the experiences into rough categories, not scientifically because we have no idea what they really are, but at least according to their apparent similarities.

We are not attempting the task in this book because there is enough of it already, but you might like to think about the idea. As you read the stories in this and the last book, try to think of what features certain stories have in common. You will find for example, that some ghosts interact with people to the extent of touching or speaking to them or doing things to annoy them. Many ghosts do not interact, they seem to be simply visions of past events in which the observer plays no part. Another distinction may be between benign and malign ghosts, those that people feel comfortable with and those they find frightening.

You will not find classifying paranormal events an easy thing to do, and we will not be able to swop correspondence with you about it, but it might be interesting. In the previous book we discussed some theories about the nature of ghosts, and (naturally) recommend you to read it. Here we have added just occasional comments on the stories and noted some theories which may explain particular events.

"Do you believe in ghosts?" is a common question, but it is a wrong and inappropriate one. First, it lumps together the dissimilar things we mentioned above. Secondly, it is a loaded question. You would not ask someone if they believed in cows or traffic lights. They are objective realities for which there is plenty of evidence. We only talk about "belief" when we are discussing ideas and values, such as morals and religious faith, where evidence is beside the point. When the issue is whether or not an event occurred or an object exists, we can only say what evidence there is and what it suggests. If we say we "believe" that a certain thing exists or happened, we don't mean that we have faith that it did, but that there is enough evidence to say so, in other words, we "think".

Those who dismiss and exclude the possibility of any truth in what people have to say about their ghostly experiences should, perhaps, examine their motives. Are they *anxious* to dispose of these puzzles and trying to bring what is strange and inexplicable into the area of the ordinary and the understood? If the idea that paranormal phenomena really do occur causes anxiety to some people, is it caused by fear of things not understood and under control? This would not be surprising because from the earliest times human beings were frightened into superstitious awe by lightning and eclipses of the sun and moon. But it just as superstitious to dismiss all evidence which seems to point to a conclusion we can't accept or explain.

In *Midland Ghosts & Hauntings* we had a chapter of advice for people who are frightened or disturbed by paranormal activity; again, you must read it. Here we have added a section for people who are intrigued by the subject and want to study it. For their benefit we have described in detail how to set up a 'ghost watch' to observe and record paranormal phenomena.

As in *Midland Ghosts etc,* most of the stories in this book are contemporary accounts of strange encounters by Midlanders in all walks of life. If the book has any value it is not because of our views or theories, but in the repeated evidence of a wide range of events that do not appear to obey the rules which science has taught us. If you already accept that what people loosely call ghosts exist, then here is evidence to help you confound the sceptics. If you are a sceptic, perhaps this selection of statements may convince you.

The accounts in this book come from a circle of about 50 miles around Birmingham, which includes every kind of community from tiny villages to crowded inner city streets. This is the heart of the most haunted islands in the world where one tenth of our population live. You will see that ghosts occur all over that area, from lonely disused airfields in the Trent Valley to the back streets of the Black Country, from stately homes and quiet villages in Warwickshire and Worcestershire to the heart of Birmingham.

Finally, our great thanks to the many, many people who have shared their experiences with us. Most of you were happy to let us print your names, but others preferred to be anonymous, so for them we have invented new names and shown this by a *. We have been able to use only a selection of their stories and if yours is not here, sorry. It doesn't mean that we did not find it interesting, just that we had far more material than we could put into a book of this size. Whether your story is here or not, without the help of people all over the Midlands this book would never have been written.

Anne Bradford and
Barrie Roberts
1997

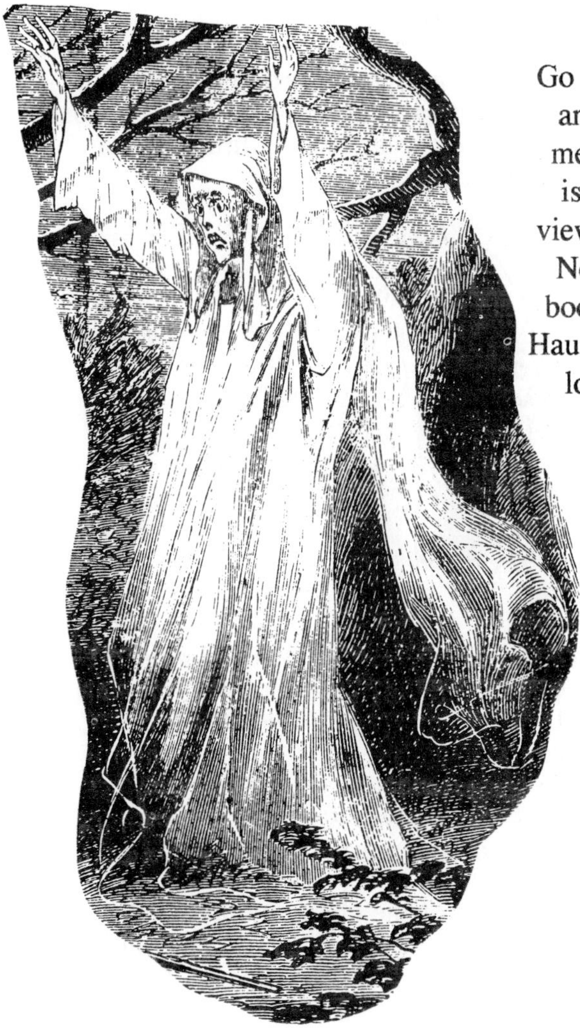

Go walking near Stourbridge and his is what you could meet - see page 9. But this is an artist's imaginative view of what ghosts are like. None of the stories in this book or `Midland Ghosts & Hauntings' suggest that ghosts look or behave like this.

Birmingham

The Old Man in Pince Nez

(City Centre)

Ron Griffin says:

"In 1948 I was a drama student in Birmingham. The school used a large flat over Mason's shop in Broad Street for scene painting and rehearsing. It stood almost opposite the Royal Orthopaedic Hospital. Entrance to the house, which was late 18th century, was by a side door which led into an entry, then up several flights of stairs. The main room was oblong and the only furnishing a few chairs, an ideal atmosphere for working.

One evening I stayed over to go through my acting examination pieces. I began my piece, but halfway through I felt that someone was watching me. Standing in the corner I saw a little old man with white hair and pince nez spectacles.

I felt myself go cold but plodded on with my piece hoping the apparition would go away. I kept my eyes on the wall trying to avoid his stare. I dreaded coming to the end, knowing that the old man would still be there.

Just as I finished the vision faded away. I switched off the light, dashed out of the room and fled downstairs into the street.

When I mentioned this to the rest of the class, another student, Bill, said that he had also seen the old man. He had been making tea in the kitchen when he heard footsteps on the stairs leading to an attic. He went to see who was there and saw the old man disappear into the large rehearsal room.

Bill made some enquiries at the shop below. He was told that the old man was an artist and a contemporary of Sir Edward Burne Jones, the Birmingham pre Raphaelite painter. The flat had once been the old man's studio and it is said that he hanged himself from a beam in the attic.

However, the old man might have brought me good luck, for the following morning I took my examination in London and passed".

Walking Round the Table

(Balsall Heath)

John Williams is Liverpool born and bred but moved to Birmingham just after the Second World War in search of work. There were plenty of jobs and he worked in factories and on building sites before marrying and settling down here.

"When I first came to Birmingham I was staying in digs at Goose Street, Highgate, Balsall Heath. All that has gone now. It was a very old house; you went up the stairs and there were three bedrooms. An Irish chap was living in another of the rooms.

One night, I was fast asleep in bed when at three o'clock in the morning, this terrible noise woke me up. It sounded as if someone was kicking at the wooden bedroom door, which was parallel to the bed, with hobnailed boots. The noise frightened the life out of me. There was another man sleeping in the room but he didn't hear it; he was fast asleep and snoring.

I sneaked out of the room and looked down the stairs. Everything was quiet and very dark. Then I saw an old woman walking slowly round the table. She was about seventy, with long grey hair and wore a white nightdress that went down to her toes. Then she just went. I was not frightened. I was more curious than anything.

The next day I was talking to the other chap in my room who said that there had been another man in the house, but he had left the previous week. I asked why and he said, 'He said he had seen a ghost'".

The Haunted Bed
(Bordesley Green)

Mrs Price* lived in a house in Bordesley Green from the early 1960s until 1997. It was at first council owned but later bought by Mr and Mrs Price. Although the house was an ordinary semi detached, many unusual incidents took place. Mrs Price's son Peter describes one of them.

"When I was only 18 I had an experience that nearly frightened me to death. I was lying in bed just before midnight when I felt a rumbling in my stomach which seemed to take over my whole body, then I felt myself lifted off the bed and moving along. I shared a room with my two younger brothers and I tried to shout out, but I could not move. I felt that if I didn't stop and fell to the floor I would die. I managed to put my foot out against my brother's bed and this stopped me going forward any more. I couldn't say how long this lasted. My mother heard a bang and rushed upstairs to find the bed across the other side of the room and upside down, as if it had been slammed on the floor".

Mrs Price gives more details:

"It was a long time ago and it is rather difficult to remember all the incidents now, but my husband used to say, 'Fred's out again!'. The lights would flash on and off and footsteps went up and down the stairs and across the landing. I used to think that the children were out of bed, but when I went to look they would all be fast asleep. The front door knob used to twist right round by itself but there was never anyone there.

Things went missing. My husband had all his records on a stand and I can remember him searching for one particular record. I knew that it had been there only a day or two before and I told him that nobody had borrowed it, but he gave up and sat down. A minute or two later I looked at the records, and there was the one he had been looking for sticking out by about two inches. He said, 'How could that happen, I've only just been through them.'

We had been there about ten years when my eldest daughter (who was married by then) came to visit me. Suddenly, a radio on the corner of the mantelpiece picked itself up and moved to the middle of the wooden surround of the gas fire. It didn't fall, it could not have fallen like that, it actually picked itself up.

I had six children and my eldest son, Peter, seemed to attract strange incidents. They always happened when he was around, and the worst things used to happen around his bed. Although the bed was second hand, it had never actually been used when we had it. My sister used to help an elderly lady who asked her to buy a new bed, but the old lady died before it was even unwrapped. I bought it for Peter but occasionally it would tip up and throw him out. We put this down to the old lady not wanting him to sleep in it.

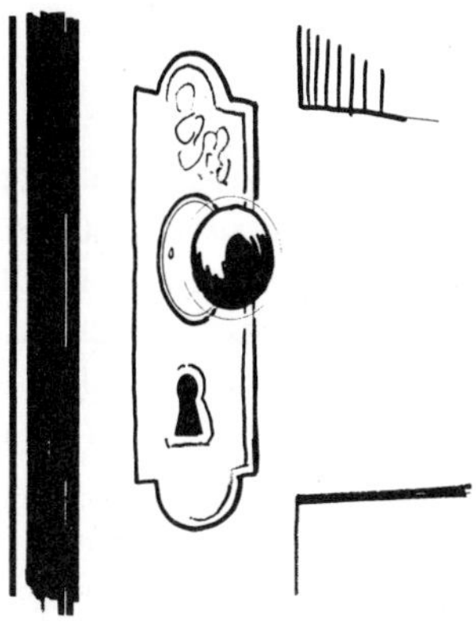

Peter slept in a room with his two younger brothers. They once had a friend to stay who said that, in the middle of the night, he saw the knob of the bedroom door turning round. I told him that the knob had come off years before. However, he was adamant that that was what he had seen and he refused to sleep in the room again.

One night when Peter was about 18, I heard a terrible noise upstairs. Peter was shouting and there was a loud banging. I ran upstairs and I found his bed had been moved and tipped right over. His younger brothers said that they had seen him with his feet sticking from the end of the bed and something was pulling him up by them."

After Peter left home there was the occasional strange incident, when something would go missing or turn up in an unexpected place, but these eventually died away and everything returned to normal. As for Peter, wherever he goes he seems to attract something. In his last flat he caught a glimpse of a woman in a flowered wrap over apron standing by his sink. Some weeks later his girlfriend was chatting to the neighbours when she mentioned this, giving all the details. They said she had described exactly the woman who had lived in the flat before them, who had been accidentally gassed.

The Lady of the Loo
(Bournville)

Bournville is, of course, the home of Cadbury's chocolate. You might believe that the spotless cleanliness of a big food manufacturing plant would discourage ghosts, but for many years there have been tales of a ghost in a ladies' toilets at Cadbury's. Jane Simpson*, now retired and living in Solihull, vouches for its existence.

"I worked at Cadbury's for thirty years, eventually becoming a manager. In about 1985 a girl who worked there was telling everyone that she had seen a female ghost in the ladies' loos in the office block. This young lady had a fiery temperament and, as I was one of the few female managers at that time, it fell to my lot to take her to task over it. I told her to calm down and not be so fanciful.

About two years later I was going to the ladies' when I saw in front of me a female dressed in black. I thought that she was wearing a black blouse and a fairly long black skirt (below the knee) with dark hair in a rather indeterminate hairstyle, probably a bun or a French pleat. I was about six steps behind and the door had closed behind her, but I pushed it open and followed her in. The ladies' was quite a large room, brightly lit, with eight or ten cubicles along one side and a row of sinks down the middle. All the cubicle doors were open and I could see that the room was empty.

I stood in the middle of this room and I spoke to the ether. I said, 'If there is anyone in here, please say so, I'm not frightened of you, please manifest yourself.'. One of my colleagues came in and asked what on earth I was doing. I said to her, 'Do me a favour, will you? Can you check each one of these cubicles and make certain that they are empty?' So she and I worked our way through all the cubicles and no one was there.

One of the girls in a neighbouring office often wore black and was rather similar in appearance to the apparition, so I thought that it could have been her. I went off to find her to see if she could throw any light on the matter, but she was wearing a bright turquoise blouse. I said to her, 'Have you been dressed like that all day?', to which she laughed and answered, 'Of course I have.'

I went back to my office saying 'That's very peculiar'. We all joked about it and said what a good job it was that the woman didn't choose the men's loos. The loos have all been changed now and rebuilt so I think it unlikely that any lady using them today will have a surprise visitor."

Midnight Tea

(Edgbaston)

City Road runs between Dudley Road and Sandon Road, and at the junction with Portland Road is a set of traffic lights. Set right on the corner is a large house. In about 1981 it had just become vacant and was being rented out as flats, when John Chapman and his girlfriend moved in.

"The only occupants were my girlfriend and myself, and a lady with a small boy aged 5. We each chose our rooms and we all wanted the first floor. The lady with the child chose a lounge and a large hallway which had been converted into a bedroom. My girlfriend and I chose a room adjoining the hallway plus another room.

A problem arose because none of the internal doors had locks so there was no way in which we could secure the door between our adjoining bedrooms. Our neighbour solved this by pushing her bed up against the door on the one side, while we pushed our wardrobe against it on the other.

The kitchen was on the ground floor with a cooker at each end and was shared by both families. We all lived happily together. One evening we were all going to the kitchen along the ground floor hallway, happily talking and laughing, when the ironing board picked itself up from the wall, flew down the kitchen towards us and smashed against the wall right in front of us. It was all over in a second or two.

We were a bit surprised but took that in our stride and said, 'Fine' and, 'Very nice', but other strange things started to happen. The kettle would switch on and start boiling for no reason. We would wake up in the middle of the night and say, 'What's that noise?' and 'Who's making tea at this time of night?'

Then our co-tenant told us that at night, when she was lying in bed, she would see a strange female walk through her bed, through the door at the back of her bed and into our bedroom. I'm glad to say that we never saw her.

I must say that I was quite relieved when we were able to leave there and move into our own house which, thankfully, was free of any unusual activity. Most of the house on City Road has now been converted into offices. I often wonder if the computer operators ever have an unfamiliar lady walking through their machines".

Walking in the Park
(Erdington)

Pype Hayes Hall is a 17th century mansion known locally as 'Lady Bagot's House'. The grounds are now a well wooded public park and golf course, but when this incident occurred the house was being used as a children's home.

As dusk fell one summer evening in 1970, three figures could be seen struggling through the park, apparently trying to hide the heavy bag they were carrying. They glanced round frequently and were obviously up to no good. Martin Brookes tells all:

"The two men, my uncle and his friend, Mr Raven, had taken me, then a small boy, out for a spot of illicit metal detecting. This was banned in the park but the banks of Plants Brook were particularly rich in finds. The detector was hidden in a large bag which we carried between us.

We had finished our work and were creeping home through the open part of the park when my uncle whispered, 'Look at that silly woman walking through the park in her nighty.' About 50

feet away was a woman about the same age as my mother, with long dark hair tied up on top and a floor length white silk dress. The neckline was square shaped and round her neck was a choker of black ribbon, below which was hanging a silver locket. We all saw her quite clearly and began to laugh quietly.

The woman was on our left and between us were some bushes which obscured her from our view for a few seconds. When we passed the bushes and looked across to see her again, she had disappeared. We stopped laughing.

We were surprised but did not think much of it until the next week, when my uncle was having a drink in the Bagot Arms and happened to mention the incident. He was told that we were among the many people who had seen the ghost of Lady Bagot. She lived at the Hall during the last century, but was murdered one evening while taking her dogs for a walk in the grounds".

Footsteps on the Stair

(Hockley)

Birmingham's post war development demolished half of Bridge Street West, Hockley, including number 1/351 which had been occupied by Mr and Mrs White*.

"We had just got married in 1952 and it was our first house. It was in a poor state, but we decorated and made it look very nice.

Every Saturday night my husband's brother and his wife used to come over to play cards and listen to Jack Jackson on the radio. One winter's evening, just after they had left, I went up to bed leaving Alan to bank up the fire ready for the next. morning. I had just got into bed when he came pounding up the stairs looking deathly white and shaking like a leaf. Apparently, he had started to climb the stairs, but as he reached the third step, footsteps had come from the bottom and run past him, he had felt the vibration. The footsteps went on to the top. Nothing else happened so he began to think he had imagined it - until the next Saturday when the whole sequence happened again. On the following Monday he took the day off work and rigged up a two way light on the stairs. That seemed to do the trick and he had no more strange experiences.

Some months later he bought the *Birmingham Evening Mail* on the way home from work. Inside was an account of a man who had been sentenced for strangling his wife. This man had been sitting in a local pub when he heard that his wife had been two timing with a neighbour, so he rushed home and up the stairs to the bedroom where he murdered her. The address was 1/351 Bridge Street West."

The Housekeeper's Room
(Moseley)

"As a child I lived in Moseley, in a lovely Georgian house with Victorian extensions. I was the eldest of three sisters and I also had a brother who was twelve years younger. My brother's room was the old housekeeper's room. He often used to talk about the lady who came to visit him in the night, and visitors to the house who slept in that room used to mention that they had seen someone. We had two or three staff who also saw her.

I slept on the third floor, but in winter I used to move into my brother's bedroom which tended to be warmer. I regularly saw this lady who came into the room at night. One just woke up and there she was. She would walk in and stand there with her hands clasped in front of her stomach. I was only young so she appeared to me to be quite elderly, but I would say in her 40s or 50s. She was of a comfortable build, slightly plump, and gave an overall impression of not quite grey - a donkey brown greyness. She wore a little cap and a chatelaine (keys and scissors) hanging from her waist. She just used to stand there and smile at you until she disappeared; she was quite benign. One just blinked and spoke to her, but she did not reply.

I lived in the house for many years and I saw her regularly right up until my marriage in 1968. I got used to her being around and she never troubled me, though visitors were alarmed.

We also had a noise in the kitchen that went on all the time. The dog would bark and it would be quite a nuisance. It sounded as if someone was rattling the pots and pans, all hustle and bustle, being very busy about things, but when you went into the kitchen nothing had been moved. We just used to shout 'Shut up!' and it would stop. My mother enjoyed having a ghost and used to tell the story with great glee".

Sarah (Northfield)

"When my mother and father separated, my sister and I went to live with my mother in a small, old house at Northfield, just to the north of Hollymoor Hospital. So many strange incidents took place that we eventually had to have the house exorcised.

My mother had the first experience. One morning she woke up and the birthday cards that she had arranged on a shelf in her bedroom were lying all over her bed. The card on top, which was from a friend named Sarah, looked as if it had been carefully opened and placed there.

My sister was playing on waste ground opposite the house when she saw someone standing in the window. The image was hazy but she could see it was female, pretty and feminine with big dark eyes, long straight hair of a most unusual bright ginger and a cream dress with a low neckline. She ran across the road to see who it was, but of course, the house was empty.

To begin with, I just felt uneasy in the house, but one night, I had an experience which still makes me feel creepy. I was about 14 and my favourite book was a large, heavy encyclopaedia about pets and animals, which I had left open on my desk in the room next to my bedroom. I was lying in bed but was definitely not asleep when I heard the pages of my book turning noisily, as if someone was reading it with some impatience, then I heard the book put down with a bang, as if he or she had finished with it. That was one of the worst experiences of my life, it was really horrible. Cold sweat was just pouring off me and I could feel my heart pounding fast. I got out of bed and ran downstairs but I dared not look into the room as I passed it.

Every time I went upstairs I felt as if someone was waiting for me on the landing. I did not tell anyone. When I wanted to go upstairs I would wait until someone else was going up and then follow them. After we had lived in the house for some months we began to hear about its past from the neighbours. A former tenant was a 19 year old named Sarah who had killed her baby on the waste ground opposite, then returned to the house and hanged herself on the landing. The house was exorcised by a team of people who said that the house had been haunted by a young girl called Sarah, but that she had now moved away. It seemed to have worked, because we had no more problems".

Stephanie Gets Things Moving
(Northfield)

Patricia Rankin* writes:

"There are five children in our family. I have an older sister, a twin brother, a younger brother and a younger sister, Stephanie. Although I am twelve years older than my younger sister, we were very close and we used to share a bedroom at our home in Northfield, but when she was 11 I got married. My mother said that my sister missed me terribly, especially when everyone else left home and she was the only one left. I used to visit whenever I could, but a couple of years later I had my first baby and I could not go so often.

One afternoon in September 1976 I phoned Mum to tell her I was coming, but instead of being pleased she said, 'Don't come round. Don't come round.' I wondered what on earth was going on.

Evidently, they had a poltergeist. Things were flying everywhere, even Mum's false teeth. Potatoes were jumping up and down in the saucepan, lights were going on and off. My mother's watch went missing and then dropped into her lap; a glass ashtray disappeared and suddenly fell on the floor. Marbles bounced down the stairs from nowhere and hit the front door. Dad used to collect them and put them in a dish in his greenhouse. He once went into my sister's bedroom and found that talcum powder had been tipped everywhere. He noticed that the room was very cold.

There was banging right through the house. My mother was worried about the neighbours complaining so one morning she asked her neighbour, 'Did you hear a lot of banging in our house last night?', but the neighbours had heard nothing.

Bedclothes were being pulled off the bed at night so my mother put strings across the bedroom. She said 'We'll find out what's pulling the bedclothes off us', but the clothes were still removed and the strings stayed intact.

The poltergeist didn't stop when visitors came. My older brother put his cigarettes on the table and every time he picked up the packet some were missing, then they came flying back across the room one by one. Mum said, 'What are you doing, throwing your cigarettes around?' He said, 'It's not me.'. My older sister told me, 'You won't believe this, I couldn't believe it myself but I saw a tomato come through the ceiling.'. When my little girl was nine weeks old I went to visit. Her dummy was on the table but it kept moving round. I said, 'How's that happening?'.

My mother was so worried that she phoned my husband and asked him to come round. At first, he thought it was all a joke and said that he did not believe any of it, but he came back petrified. As he had walked down the stairs, stones had been thrown at him from behind, hitting him in the back.

I said to Mum, and at another time to my Dad, 'Come over to my house and have a break from it.', but they would not leave each other alone and they would not leave Stephanie.

Stephanie was the only person who was calm about all this. For example, when the lights went off one evening my parents thought it was a power cut and were flapping around. Stephanie went outside and saw that everybody else's lights were on. She said, 'What's all the panicking about?' and sat on the settee as calm as anything. Then the lights came on again. The fusebox was in the pantry and could not have been touched because there was black tape round it which was still intact.

One day, both Mum and Dad distinctly heard someone making loud sucking noises, licking their lips and cracking something with their teeth. This, and the fact that ornaments were flying round, made my Dad think that all these events was caused by my Mum's parents returning to haunt us. My grandfather had been fond of mints and he loved ornaments - he had put them all round his garden pool.

Dad kept saying, 'You shouldn't have buried those two together in the same grave, they never got on and now they're throwing things at each other in our house.'

My mother began to suspect that it was something to do with Stephanie because things only happened in the house while she was there. In addition, every night when my sister went to sleep, the whole house started vibrating so that everything trembled.

After about three months my mother had proof that Stephanie was the cause of the disturbances. She had gone to bed and was asleep with Mum lying by her side. Suddenly, the bed covers began coming off and going up and down. By the side of Stephanie's bed was one of those large, toy snakes which were popular at one time, made from fluffy fabric with a red felt tongue. Stephanie slowly raised her hands in the air and the snake was moving in and out of her fingers. The next morning Mum phoned me up and said, 'I think there's something wrong with your sister.'

It was when the glass panel in the kitchen door smashed that Mum got really worried. It just shattered one evening while she was working in the kitchen. When the relatives came they said, 'What's happened to your kitchen door?' but she would not tell them the truth, she said that the wind had blown it in.

At this point Mum went crying to the local vicar and asked him to come and bless the house. The vicar did come but things got worse. Even as he was blessing the house things were moving round. He advised my mother to see a Spiritualist.

Mum went with Stephanie to see two Spiritualists, a man and a women. She told me later that it had been a terrible scene. They sat my sister in the chair and were shouting, 'Leave her alone!' while Mum sat in the background, sobbing. They told Mum that the sort of things we had experienced can happen when children are at puberty. Their advice was that Mum should let Stephanie stay at home and keep her quiet. Things would continue to happen but they would slow down and it would take four sessions to cure her.

After that my sister seemed to be in a trance, as if she did not care what happened. She stared at people in a strange way and frightened quite a few.

Afterwards Mum found out that she had been having problems at school; she had not long changed from the junior to the comprehensive school and was being bullied. Mum kept her at home for a bit and by the end of three weeks, the paranormal activity had died away.

The Spiritualists had said that it could occur at any time in the future, and in 1980 my sister was treated for anxiety attacks and given tranquillisers".

Patricia correctly identifies the phenomenon as a poltergeist and its centre as her young sister. Poltergeist is German for 'noisy ghost', but the name is misleading. If you believe that ghosts are something external to and independent of human beings, then poltergeists are not ghosts.

Every culture in history has recognised poltergeists. The oldest known British cases were recorded eight centuries ago by Giraldus Cambrensis (see *Midland Ghosts & Hauntings).* Wherever they occur their behaviour is very similar. They make noises, they shift objects, sometimes they start small fires, occasionally they speak, usually sarcastically or abusively. Their object seems to be to make mischief and attract attention, but for all the noise and disturbance they may cause they are harmless. They do little damage to property and never inflict serious hurt on human beings.

Some poltergeists have become very famous, like Gef the Talking Mongoose who manifested in a farmhouse at Doarlish Cashen in the Isle of Man in the 1930s, and even featured in a celebrated libel action. Then there was the Bell Witch of Tennessee a century before. The Bell Witch's fame attracted a visit from President Andrew Jackson, when it demonstrated the poltergeist's observed contempt for authority by whipping off the President's hat as he rode through the gate and skimming it in the mud.

Poltergeists almost always revolve around stressed adolescents, usually girls but occasionally boys. There are a few known cases where they have centred on older people. They seem to be an exaggerated manifestation of a stressed child's desire for attention. They are anti authoritarian and it can be extremely dangerous to confront them with authority figures like priests, exorcists, spiritualists and psychiatrists. They are not 'evil spirits', if such things exist, and the treatment applied in the above case was not only inappropriate, it was dangerous.

Not the least interesting interesting thing about poltergeists is the mechanism by which they produce these astonishing physical effects. Clearly some assembly, direction and discharge of energy occurs, but no one understands its nature or how it is controlled.

Through the Living Room
(Sheldon)

Live people do not walk through walls, do they? So what did Peter see?

"What I'm telling you now happened round about 1975 or 1976 when I was in my mid 20s, and it is something that I have never forgotten. I left work at about 2 o'clock on a Friday afternoon and a friend dropped me at my flat in Sheldon. My wife had gone to her mother's, so I was alone. It was a nice, sunny afternoon and I was sitting on the settee in the living room, when, at about 4 o'clock, a man appeared through one wall, walked across the room and out through the wall the other side.

He was quite elderly, about 65 or 70, and he was very tall and smart, with a brown, pin striped suit and grey hair combed back. He looked very real, except that he was slightly transparent. I did not know him but I would recognise him if I saw him again. Our living room is quite a long room and he walked diagonally across it, taking no notice of me at all. It was all over in about twenty seconds".

Riders in the Dusk
(Sutton Park)

Bishop Vesey persuaded Henry VIII to present Sutton Park to the town in 1528. The line of the old Roman Road, Icknield Street, runs along the Park's western edge of where it touches the Chester Road, though there is nothing to be seen on the ground. The Chester Road was one of the three worst in the Midlands for highway robbery between the mid 17th and late 18th centuries. One of the most notorious highwaymen was Tom King, one time partner of Dick Turpin. He was born locally near Stonnal, and probably burnt to death in the Park for his crimes.

Local legend has it that a ghostly highwayman rides at dusk from Rowton's Well in the middle of the southern half of the park, crosses Icknield Street and the Chester Road into Sutton Oak Road, and then heads for the Parson & Clerk public house. Many local people walking their dogs in the evening and several courting couples claim to have have seen him. The highwayman appears to be youngish, although his face cannot be seen clearly because of a mask. He wears a tricorn hat and a black cape, and rides a large bay horse with a black mane and tail.

A second phantom was seen in November 1992 by a park ranger.

"I was riding round the pool one evening at dusk on my motor bike in order to lock up. I was going away from Powell's Pool towards Banner's Gate to lock up the gate there, when I saw a man on a white horse riding through the trees of Westwood Coppice. I rode towards him to tell him that the park was closing and that the area was considered unsafe for horse riders, but he disappeared into the woods. I scoured the woods but no one could be found. I radioed for a second ranger but neither of us could find anyone.

I saw the rider quite clearly. His clothes were of a silky material and he was not wearing a riding hat. His riding boots were full length, coming right up the back of his calf and his saddle was of a Western type with a high back and pommel".

Westwood Coppice

Heathland in Sutton Park

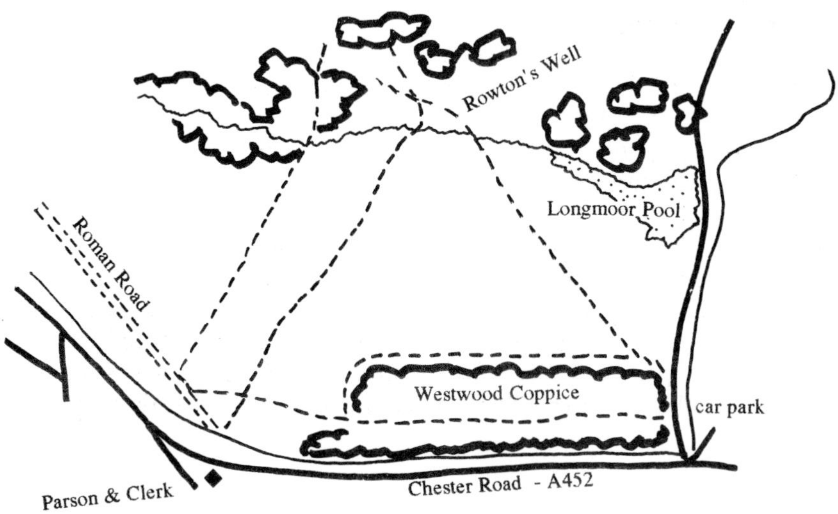

The Vanishing Victim
(Witton)

David Bingham made headlines in the *Birmingham Evening Mail* on 2nd January 1996 when his car hit something strange:

"I'm under a plumbing contract to Birmingham City Council and on a 24 hour call out. Early this morning I finished a job at Kingstanding, and at 10 to 1 I was driving back from Kingstanding to Witton, making my way to Aston where I was lodging temporarily with a relative. I took a short cut down Moor Lane beside Witton Cemetery, when suddenly, about 150 yards from the junction with Brookvale Road, this bloke appeared. He was an ordinary looking man in his late forties with short black hair, a long black jacket and black trousers. In the split second that he appeared, my car hit him. As it hit him, he looked up at me, and I can't get the look in those eyes out of my head. There was a solid thud as he hit the front of the bonnet. I slammed the anchors on and jumped out of the van, expecting the worst, but there was nothing on the road. I looked everywhere, under the van - everywhere, but I couldn't find anything.

I got back into the van and went as fast as I could to my mate's house a short distance away, and we phoned the police. They came straight out and interviewed me. We all went out and looked around but nothing was there. The strange thing was that there was not even a mark on the van.

People say that I saw a bit of fog or a snowman but that's ridiculous. I know what I saw and I heard that thump as it hit the bonnet".

A Horrible Low Laugh
(Yardley)

In the 1960s the old shops and houses in the centre of Yardley were demolished to make way for the new Tivoli Shopping Centre with some flats. About twelve years later, Sue King* moved into one of the two bedroomed flats.

"In 1974 I was working at Butlins as a red coat, and as our organist needed overnight accommodation, I let him sleep at my flat one night. When he left he said, 'I don't want to worry you but there's something in your flat. While I was here I felt as if eyes were following me everywhere, and I have never felt like that before.'

Nothing much out of the ordinary happened until I moved my bedroom because of damp. The next morning, I woke up at 6 to find it was already light. As I turned over and pulled up the quilt I felt someone come into the room. I looked up and no one was there, but I could feel it coming over to my bed. Suddenly, I felt a heavy weight, like a man's body, climb onto the bed and crawl on top of me though I could still see nothing. I heard this horrible, low laugh and something like a pillow was pushed into my face. I could not breathe and I could not move to push it away. I felt paralysed, my muscles had frozen. I thought, 'I'm going to die, oh please God help me.' I suppose I was only suffocating for a minute or two, but it seemed a long time before the pillow was removed and the weight went. I got off the bed, shaking, but I could still feel a presence in the room.

Then my small son, who was then about two years old, toddled into the bedroom and said, 'Mummy, there's a man in my eyes.' He seemed very frightened.

My mother came round in the morning and found me in a terrible state, I cried as I told her what had happened. I never discovered what it was all about and changed my accommodation as soon as I could".

★

The little boy's phrase is so strange that he is most unlikely ever to have heard anyone else use it. It must be his attempt to describe literally what he experienced. What does it suggest? It might be an apt way to describe something which was visible but not solid, perhaps misty or wraith like.

"My Flat is Haunted."

(Erdington)

Suzie* Edwards talks about life in her flat.

"There is no doubt that my flat is haunted. All kinds of strange things happen. The handles turn on the bathroom and bedroom doors. The light bulbs keep popping, one after the other. I lose things and they turn up in strange places. For example a blue hairbrush which I keep in my handbag has turned up on top of the bathroom cabinet. No way would I put a hairbrush up there. When I come back from a walk the first thing I always do is put the keys by the telephone with the dog lead. I have found the keys in all kinds of peculiar places, such as on the bedroom dressing table or in the kitchen, when I have not been there. I have been lying on the settee when someone has thumped the armchair next to it. My front door scrapes on the floor and you have to yank to open it, but the other week I went to go through and it opened all by itself for me, quite smoothly and without any scraping. I have felt someone tapping me, and at night I can hear heavy breathing as if someone is walking round my bed.

A lot of the paranormal activity is centred in the bathroom. I have been in there when the light pull has suddenly started swinging for no reason; there was no draught or anything. Recently I saw the bath tidy across the bath lifted up at one end and carefully replaced. Then clicking noises come from the washing basket. I have emptied it and looked through the contents but found nothing there which could produce a click. I leave my nightdress folded nicely on the washing basket while I have a bath. A short time ago the sleeve lifted itself up and then placed itself down again. The mirror is on a swivel which is very stiff and difficult to turn. I know that when I go out of the bathroom I always leave it tilted upwards, so does Keith, my husband, because he is very tall. But often when I go back it is tilted downwards, completely the opposite way.

Things happen in the kitchen too. For no reason a knife will start spinning round. In the night when we're in bed we can hear the bread bin opening and shutting. A couple of times I have had my bum pinched when I was bending down.

I was in bed early in the morning a few weeks ago when my husband said to me,

"You'd better wake up, I think there's something wrong with your neighbour". I sat up to hear a loud tap, tapping on our bedroom wall, which adjoins the house of our elderly next door neighbour. I grabbed my dressing gown and shot round to her house. Everything was quiet. I shouted through the letter box, asking if she was alright. She came to the front door, saying 'I'm alright, what's wrong?' I said that something had been tapping my wall. She said, 'It wasn't me, I've only just got up.' Keith said it must have been a bird on the roof. I have never heard a bird sound like that before.

Two or three months ago I saw some kind of apparition in the little passageway inside my front entrance door. It was just a whitish grey shape of a lady, like a net curtain. I could not see the head or the arms, just the body. I only saw it for a few seconds but I had the impression that it was someone of average build but quite old. She was wearing a dress and had very large shoulders, as if it had puffed sleeves or something.

Other people have had strange experiences here. My mother had been relaxing on the settee when someone has raised her head. My nephew is now aged 13, but when he was 7 or 8 he was sleeping on the camp bed when something lifted him up and threw him through the air so that he landed at the bottom of the bed. Fortunately he didn't seem to wake up properly, so I managed to comfort him while he was still half asleep.

In 1993 my Aunt Janet came down without her husband. My husband was having to take O and A levels for his job and he was finding the theory difficult. Janet had passed these exams many years before, so she came over to help him. They sat on the settee and I was sitting beside them, when suddenly we heard a rustling from a carrier bag in the corner, which was full of junk. Next morning, when I took her a first cup of tea, Janet said she couldn't stay any longer. She had been sleeping on the settee and the carrier bags had continued to rattle away under the table though there was nothing alive in them and the dog was in another room. Then, in the middle of the night, something large and black had risen off the table. I told her not to be silly, it was only the cat, but she said that it definitely wasn't. Finally, she had been frightened by a very vivid dream, where she felt that she was rising up off the bed, still in a horizontal position, travelling through the wall and floating through different rooms.

About twelve months ago I was temporarily looking after a valuable antique rocking chair, a family heirloom. My nephew was staying with me at the time and he would keep sitting on it and rocking it. I kept saying to him, 'Get off that chair and come and sit on the settee.'. I went out for a short while and when I came back he was ashen faced. He said, 'Get that rocking chair out of here, please.' He had been rocking in the chair when someone had said 'Boo!' to him.

Another young nephew came to live with me for six or seven months when he was 5. He reckoned that he could see this ghost and described it in some detail. It was a tubby man in his 50s, getting thin on top and wearing a leather jacket. This sounded just like my cat's previous owner, Harry, a stacker truck driver with whom I used to work. He had died a few years previously and I had adopted his cat.

Every Wednesday evening, my family arrives and we have a film night. On one of these Wednesdays I was standing in the middle of the living room when a flash of red light appeared behind me, it went round my body, up to my husband who was sitting on the settee, and out through the window. Dad said, 'My God, what was that?' Whatever it was, it seemed to be having a go at my husband, perhaps it didn't approve of our relationship.

Recently my husband, who tends to pooh pooh everything, was standing in the middle of the room when the television suddenly turned itself on. The remote control was on the top of the settee and no one was near it. Another time I was in bed in the middle of the night and I could hear the video tape running. The tape would stop, wind itself back, start running, stop, and go back. I told my husband that I had heard the tape working in the night and he scoffed, but when he went to play it that evening it was in a terrible mess. He said, 'What have you been doing to this tape?' The beginning was at the back, the middle of the film was at the front and so on. He said there was something wrong with our video. Well, there was never anything wrong before and there has not been since.

I'm not at all afraid of these spirits or whatever they are, in fact I quite like them. I feel that they're the people I once knew and was very fond of. One of them, I'm sure, is my gran. Sometimes I can feel something stroking my hair, just as gran did when she was alive. Occasionally, I can smell her perfume".

★

The flash of red light that moved about may have been some form of what is called 'ball lightning'. It does enter houses and not just through open doors or windows but through solid walls, and it does move about. Usually it moves out again, but on occasions it has been known to explode inside a building, sometimes causing serious damage. Our grandparents used to leave the doors open in thundery weather 'to let the lightning out', which seems a wise precaution.

Cold Spots and a Cavalier
(Sutton Coldfield)

A short walk uphill from Holy Trinity Church in Sutton Coldfield is the Three Tuns Inn. It has fallen victim to the fashion for changing old pubs into featureless links in a national chain and is currently called the 'Futile & Flatulent', or something. However, the old name is still spread across the front in three foot high base relief. The Tuns dates back to the 17th century and was once a coaching inn, with its bars now flanking the gateway through which coaches used to enter the yard. But the place was first important in the Civil War when it became the local headquarters of the Parliamentary army.

Beneath the pub are some peculiar cellars, which are not so much cellars as a zigzag of passages. Set in the cellar wall is a tiny arched doorway which is bricked up.

A few years ago a landlord decided to open the sealed doorway. He wanted to see if there was any truth in the local legend that there is an underground passage from the cellars to the crypt of the Church. However, the brewery were fearful that interfering with the support of the ancient building might cause it to collapse and prevented his investigations.

Local legend has it that the cellars of the Three Tuns are haunted by the ghost of a boy Cavalier. He is suppose to have been imprisoned in the cellars and died there, though another version says he was put in the stocks on the green by the church and stoned, then carried to the Three Tuns where he died. A recent landlord has described seeing the figure of a youth down in the cellars 'dressed like the Blue Boy painting'. The present staff say that, whenever they work late in the cellars on stocktaking, something puts the lights out.

The Gate is a pub which stands between the Three Tuns and the church, and its name has also been changed. However, the original name was given because it stands on the site of a tollgate at the entrance to the town. It is said that in the 1960s a misty humanoid shape was seen in the ladies toilets on the ground floor.

A previous landlady of The Gate told us:

"Our private quarters always had 'cold spots' that we could not get rid of, no matter how much additional heating we had. While I lived at The Gate, my small son developed an imaginary playmate who came into his room and talked to him. He said that he was a man with long hair and floppy clothes and my son called him Burble because he spoke in a funny way. My son also developed an aversion to the upstairs bathroom (directly above the downstairs ladies' loo) and could be quite hysterical about going into it".

She left the pub in about 1973 and shortly afterwards a ghost watch was held there which reported seeing a figure in a Cavalier costume. Could this explain the long hair and floppy clothes?

The cutting of a new road junction exposed the foundations of The Gate and revealed a walled up archway and some steps. If there ever was a tunnel from the Three Tuns to the church it would pass beneath The Gate. Perhaps there was, and perhaps the same Cavalier haunts both pubs.

The Black Country

Mrs Peters

(Smethwick)

John Cross* used to live in Windmill Lane, Smethwick until he did his National Service in the early 1950s:

"It was late when I arrived home on leave, and to get to Windmill Lane I had to walk through Victoria Park and up Ballot St, which was quite different then. On one corner was Duffields the greengrocers, there was another shop on the opposite corner, whilst halfway along the road was a little shop where I used to buy my sweets. It was run by a dear old lady by the name of Mrs Peters who was crippled. She used to have half the door folded down, like a trap door, and sit behind it selling sweets. I could see quite plainly that the shop door was open and Mrs Peters was sitting in her chair. I called out, 'Hullo Mrs Peters.' and she said 'Goodnight'.

When I got home I mentioned to my mother that I had seen the old lady and she said, 'You couldn't have done, she's been dead and buried for the last twelve months and the shop closed with her.'

Floating at the Punchbowl

(Bilston)

When the Greyhound & Punchbowl was built in 1435 it was the home of the de Bilston family and known as Stowheath Manor. The de Bilstons became the Moseleys and the Manor was sold in the 17th Century. For as long as anyone can remember it has had the reputation of being haunted, and here is Bill Bailey's* account of the ghost.

"In the 1940s, when I was 11 years old, I went with my parents to visit relations at Bilston. It was a red hot day and on the way back we called at the Greyhound & Punchbowl for a cold drink. You had to go through a long, narrow hallway to get to the counter. My parents went off to the bar while I stood in the entrance with a glass of pop. I noticed that although it was so hot, the hall was freezing cold. Then I saw, at the far end of the corridor, a white mist which floated about, forming shapes and drifting off again. As I watched, it developed into a human form, to become a lady in a long white dress, floating about.

I went out of the corridor and closed the door. Later I told my parents what I had seen but they didn't believe me. However, as I grew older and started reading the newspapers I noticed that, particularly during the 1950s and 60s, the pub was often mentioned in the *Express and Star* because a ghost had been seen there."

The Spectre of Whittington Heath
(Kinver)

The *Illustrated Police News* was a late 19th Century tabloid. Like its modern descendants it dealt in crimes, disasters and society scandals, but it did not possess their sexual freedom. Instead, it developed the dramatic possibilities of monsters and strange animals, filling its pages with gorillas, sea serpents, giant squids and elephants. It flourished years before the printing of photographs became possible, a distinct advantage because its illustrations came not from the camera lens, but from the overheated imaginations of its engravers. Another speciality was the supernatural, and on 14th December 1872 it chilled readers with the following awful tale:

'Encounter with a ghost near Brierley Hill

The following letter was addressed to the Editor of the *Brierley Hill & Stourbridge Advertiser:*

"Perhaps you will afford me space to give a short narrative of an adventure which occurred while crossing Whittington Common, which people who are acquainted with the locality know is a lonely place at night. I had been to Kinver and remained rather longer than I intended, and about half past eleven passed Whittington Inn. In two minutes or so I was in the solitude of the Common. With the silence around me I was on my guard in case I should be surprised or set upon by some desperate character, but let no one suppose I was oppressed by the silence or solitariness. No such thing. I was enjoying the solitariness and drinking delight from

From Illustrated Police News
14th December 1872

Melodrama from a Victorian magazine artist. For a similar picture from another blood and thunder publication, see "Midland Murders & Mysteries"

the wondrous beauty and calmness of the scene and jogging along at something like three miles an hour. From the time of leaving Kinver I had not met a single soul, but at this moment just as I was about to ascend a hill - I observed a figure approaching.

Its manner of approach struck me as strange, it appeared rather to glide than walk, but I accounted for this by the softness of the ground which prevented me hearing the footfalls. At this moment the moon was overshadowed and a comparative darkness fell upon the scene. There however, the figure still stood, and I could see it plainly although the moon was obscured. I demanded why I was thus stopped, but there was no answer and I made an attempt to pass on one side. I was far from feeling assured that I could force a passage and raising my stick with all my force aimed a blow at the unwelcome visitor. My blow was well aimed but my stick passed straight through what ought to have been a head. The swing made me stumble and I heard a low chuckling laugh. The figure extended a long arm and I was pressed gently but irresistibly down until I was laid upon my back on the wayside. A cold sweat broke out and the phantom continued to stand a yard away. I could see it with perfect distinction as the cloud had passed from the moon and she was again pouring a silver stream over everything around.

At last day began to break, and as the first ray gilded the clouds on the eastern horizon the phantom lifted up both its arms over its shadowy head, uttered once again its mocking chuckle, and disappeared.

I felt immediate deliverance and reached home in a complete state of exhaustion, mental and physical. I can only say that I never get drunk and was perfectly sober. Moreover, no dreams visit the bestial sleep of the drunkard. Others will say that I must be a timid man and that my imagination played me a trick. To this I would say that I am not of a timorous nature and my health was never better at the time. How to account for the adventure I cannot tell, but I shall not forget the experience of that horrible night".

Perhaps he was more timorous than he thought and the crossing of a lonely waste late at night provoked a misidentification of mist or a strange bush. Then again, had he been drinking something stronger than delight?

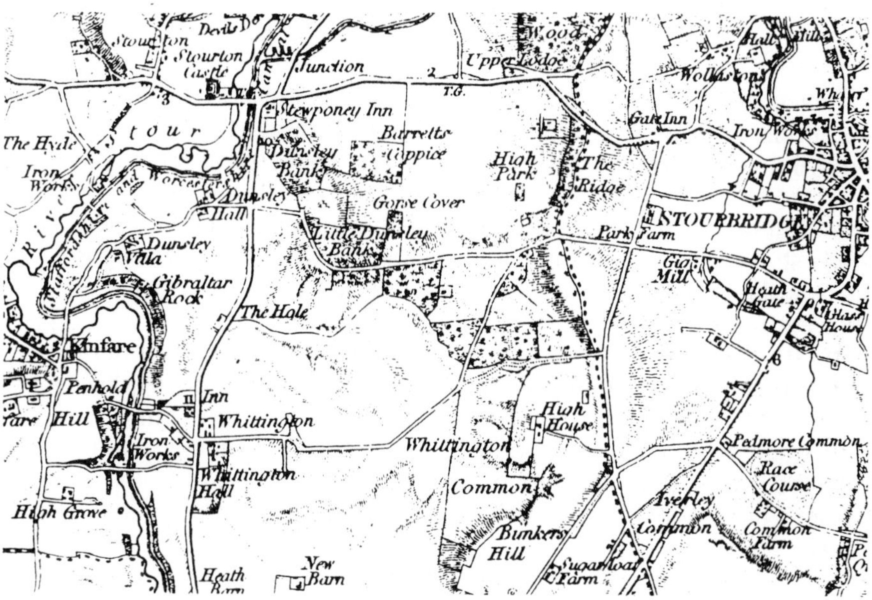

The Common is near Stourbridge rather than Brierley Hill. Local people may know it as a rolling, sandy area which until recently was a vast sewage farm. Liquid waste gurgled evilly from squat blue brick towers to spread over the land in the hope that it would vanish, or something.

The map is taken from Sheet 62 (Lichfield) of the First Series Ordnance Survey maps. It was published in 1834 at a scale of 1 inch to a mile. Those of you who know the area will spot features such as the Whittington Inn, Sugar Loaf Farm and the outline of Bunker's Hill Wood. The roads in 1834 were very much as they are now, though more of them would have been the sandy, tree lined tracks which are now bridleways.

The Grey Man
(Brierley Hill)

"I don't want my identity revealed in any way. I don't mind for myself, I don't care what my friends and neighbours say about me, but it's for the sake of my daughter. Whatever happens, she must not hear what I am going to tell you now.

I moved into this semi detached when it was new, in 1978. I can think of no reason why it should be haunted as there were no previous occupants and it was built on waste scrubland.

My daughter is now 12 years old and has spent all her life here. At first she was very happy, then when she was nine she began to complain that a man was coming into her room at night and looking round. She described him as old, with grey hair. I naturally thought that she was having nightmares and told her not to be so silly. It got to the stage where she was too frightened to go to bed, so I used to sit with her for a short time until she was settled. As soon as I left her bedroom she would pull the bedclothes over her head and start singing at the top of her voice. We could hear her singing above our television.

In the summer of 1992 I woke up one morning just as it was getting light, somewhere between half past 3 and 4 o'clock. Something caught my eye and I looked across the bedroom, to see that coming through the bedroom wall which adjoins my daughter's bedroom was an elderly man. Apart from the fact that he was walking through the wall he looked like an actual person, I could not see through him, he was quite solid. He was very ordinary looking, with grey hair and a grey suit, perhaps about 5 feet 8 inches tall, with a rather heavy build. This alarmed me so much that, since then, I have woken up every night at the same time and lain awake, waiting for him to appear, but I haven't seen him since.

My mother always said she had 'the gift' and I often wonder if I have it because I can sense things. For example I know when people are going to ring the doorbell. It would appear that my poor daughter has 'the gift' too. It is, I'm afraid, something that she will have to learn to live with".

The Second Key
(Walsall)

Gordon Thompson* is in his 50s, and has lived in Walsall for thirty five years.

"About twenty five years ago I lived in a flat in a residential street in south Walsall. For a while I shared it with a girl-friend, but she moved on.

Several months after my girlfriend, Jane, had left, I went out one night with a friend. He drove me home afterwards in his Mini and we stopped outside my front door at about 1 o'clock in the morning.

As I opened the passenger door and started to get out, I felt my bunch of keys slide out of my right hand pocket. Something fell outside the car and I heard it hit the stone kerb.

I picked up my key ring and found that one key had come loose and was missing. It was the middle of a winter's night, so it had to be my front door key that had gone.

Bob and I searched all round the car door, but found no key. I was worried, because there was a drain grill just underneath the car and I began to suspect that the key had hit the kerb and bounced into it. The front door was the only way into the flat.

We moved the car and searched again; still no key. By then I was quite sure that it had bounced into the drain. Bob said 'Do you think it might be in the car?' but I said, 'No, I heard it hit the stone kerb outside'. Nevertheless, he searched inside the car.

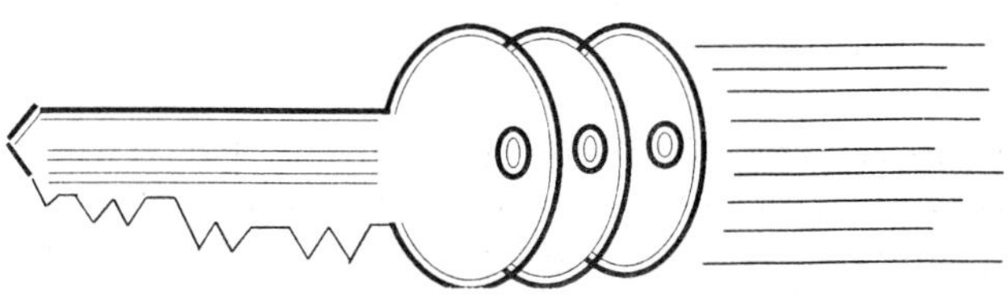

I was looking at my front door, considering ways of breaking in, when Bob said, 'There's a key here'. He had found a Yale key underneath the car's floor mat on the passenger side. I looked, but the key he had found was yellow metal and my front door key was silver.

In desperation I tried all the other Yale keys on my ring, but none of them would open my door. To my utter astonishment, Bob tried the key he had found and it opened the door. Even more astonishing, when I looked at Bob's key in the indoor light I saw that it was the duplicate that I had had made for Jane. I had marked it with a cross because she had several similar keys. The really peculiar elements of all this are that Jane had never returned her key to me, and Bob had never met her. So how did her key turn up under the mat of Bob's car just when I desperately needed it?"

★

Yes, you are going to write to the publisher saying that there is nothing very paranormal about this one, and its obvious that .... All right cynics, but even if Jane had been in Bob's car, in some capacity, why should the only object she dropped be *this* single key? The odds against what happened occurring might be even longer than those of it being some paranormal event, if we had the faintest idea what the probabilities were?

A Twisted Skein

(Walsall)

Fazal is a taxi driver who frequently works nights and lives with his wife and children in a terraced house in the Chuckery, Walsall. In the summer of 1994 a chip pan fire seriously damaged his kitchen. The insurance assessors were as mean as usual and a dispute ensued over the extent of the damage. Fazal asked a neighbour to photograph the damaged area.

"I had bought a new Kodak film for the job. My camera was relatively new and had never faulted. I went round the damaged area with Fazal, taking any pictures that I thought would illustrate the smoke and heat damage.

The kitchen is separated from the back sitting room by a small lobby, from which the stairs rise. I stood at the door of the sitting room and aimed my camera at the open kitchen door. I intended to show how the escaping heat had marked the paintwork outside the kitchen. It was daylight but dim in the little hallway, and I was using flash.

Fazal stood behind me, no one else was in the house, and neither of us was smoking. I took that picture and moved on to photograph the smoke staining on the stairs.

A few days later the prints came back. They were all perfect apart from that view of the stair lobby. Across the foreground, from lower right to upper left, is a twisted skein of something bluey white and misty, something that neither Fazal nor I saw. It appears on the negative and is not, apparently, a processing or film fault. There is every indication that the camera flash caught something that I couldn't see".

Fazal tells us that following the fire, his wife became nervous about the nights when he is out at work. Although she always locks up when he has gone, he says:

"She hears noises after she has gone to bed, as though someone has come in the back door and is going through all the internal doors of the house. She is now very careful to shut all the doors in the house before she goes to bed, but she still hears the sounds in the night and in the morning they are shut."

★

Building operations seem to disturb ghosts, but do fires? Fazal's wife started hearing the noises before the kitchen was rebuilt.

Fazal's strange photo of his stair lobby

Chucking About Time
(Dudley)

Poltergeists, we said earlier, make a lot of fuss but they don't do much harm. There are many cases of them hurling quite large objects at people which only just touch the victim when they arrive. A few years ago, though, a Dudley poltergeist seems to have broken the rules.

In 1989 Mrs Gloria Flemings was a 40 year old barmaid at the Old Priory public house in New Street, Dudley. At the time the pub seemed to be suffering a number of paranormal manifestations. Barmaid Mrs Sarah Winchurch was cut on the leg by a flying glass that came from nowhere, and another mysteriously flying glass narrowly missed her colleague, Janice Leatham. Lights and music suddenly switched themselves on in the middle of the night and a row of five glass lampshades shattered suddenly, though the bulbs inside remained intact. Part time barmaid Helen Osborne leapt to safety when an empty whiskey bottle flew over a partition and nearly hit her.

It was Mrs Flemings' experience, though, that hit the headlines. On 5th October 1989 the *Birmingham Evening Mail* ran a front page lead story under the headline, 'ATTACKED BY PUB GHOST! Barmaid sues after spook hurls a glass'.

Mrs Flemings said, "I was talking to a customer when this glass suddenly came off the shelf above the bar and struck me. It did not fall vertically, it seemed to come off at a funny angle of about 45 degrees and flew into me. I don't know if I believe in ghosts, but I can't explain it".

The manager of the Old Priory, Bob Darby, told the Mail, "It is eerie. It does not bother me personally, but I am concerned when my staff start getting hurt". He organised prayers at the pub, then called in the Reverend Michael Goss, vicar of Saint Thomas's church.

Mr Goss said, "I am totally puzzled by the odd goings on in the building. I have not performed an exorcism. I keep away from that word like the plague. If there are ghostly goings on, it would seem there might be a poltergeist involved, a mischievous spirit. I have spoken to all concerned. They are all very down to earth rational people. It defies any rational explanation".

Mrs Flemings, it seemed, had submitted a compensation claim to the pub's owners, Holt, Plant and Deakin, whose Managing Director, Graham Page, said, "I imagine Mrs Flemings would be covered by insurance".

★

Our attempts to follow up this fascinating story have reached a dead end. We could not contact Mrs Flemings, Mr Goss, or Bob Darby and the pub is under new (very recent) management. They have heard stories but had no experiences (yet).

Mr Goss seems to have been right. This was a more than usually violent poltergeist. Where a number of women work together, particularly when they are subject to either boredom or stress, paranormal effects are not uncommon. That is not a sexist comment. It has been established that more women experience psychic phenomena than men, more girls become the centres of poltergeist activity and, of course, more women were burned as witches, a peculiarity which were explored and tried to explain in *Midland Ghosts & Hauntings*. It seems to us that among the ladies working at the Old Priory in 1989 there may have been one who harboured some strong resentment against someone, perhaps one of her colleagues, and that this came out in psychic form.

It is interesting to note how unwilling the Reverend Goss was to carry out an exorcism. Priests of the Church of England and the Roman Catholic Church cannot do so without the permission of their Bishops, which is rarely granted. The ceremony is for casting out evil spirits, and if you are not sure you are dealing with an evil spirit, should not be used. Bearing in mind what we said earlier about facing poltergeists with authority figures, we hate to think what a violent poltergeist might have done if exorcism had been tried.

As to Mrs Flemings' claim against her employers, this would depend upon whether Holt, Plant & Deakin had failed in their duty to provide a safe place and safe systems of work. Paranormal events are not common in most peoples' work, so employers would have no duty to act unless they actually knew about them. If your employer's business is like that of John Wellington Wells in *The Sorcerer* by Gilbert and Sullivan the position will be different. He was a

> " .... dealer in magic and spells,
> In blessings and curses and ever filled purses,
> Auguries, witches and knells."

If employers know that dangerous events occur at a workplace, then they must take such steps to make it safe as are reasonable in the light of the likelihood of injury, and its severity if it does happen. In practice, we find it hard to imagine that any court would at present accept evidence of the paranormal, so flying bottles and glasses would be treated as ordinary accidents, the employer would be held responsible and their insurers would have to pay.

If, one day, knowledge of the paranormal increases to the extent that a court might be convinced that a poltergeist, or something, was responsible for certain events, then the employer would be judged in the light of what he could reasonably do about them. At present we have no idea what that might be, except to send for Mr Wellington Wells, but the increased knowledge of the subject might suggest precautions. We hope Mrs Flemings was compensated. We would be interested to hear of any other legal or insurance claims arising out of hauntings. We know of an American claim for loss of an arm by spontaneous human combustion, but that was proved to be fraudulent.

Coventry

The Strange Death of Mary Clues

(Dugdale)

Spontaneous combustion is the bizarre phenomenon which causes living humans to burn to death in sudden blasts of intense heat. According to many scientists it does not happen, but something remarkably like it happened to poor Mary Clues two hundred years ago.

Mary lived in Dugdale, now an area of Coventry about a mile north-west of the City centre, but then a rural valley west of the Radford Road. Mr Wilmer, the City Surgeon, was called to attend her grisly remains and found a middle aged woman whose skin, skull, breast and spine had been reduced to a chalk powder by the action of heat, and were covered with a strange white dust. Only one leg and thigh were still complete, and nothing remained of the shins, muscles or abdominal parts.

The body lay between a bed and the chimney, and Mr Wilmer was intrigued to see that imprinted on the wall was a black, charcoal shadow of the woman.

The death was discovered by two neighbours who broke down the door. As they did so a sheet of white flame went through the room. Doctor Trottor, who had made a study of spontaneous combustion, was notified and examined the remains. He said he had come across several examples and that each had been "inordinately addicted to strong drink and always females of an advanced age".

★

Three hundred years ago there were doctors who had seen "several examples" and had studied the subject. Now we have scientists who have seen no examples but deny the existence of spontaneous human combustion. Nevertheless, there are policemen and firemen and doctors and journalists (and even one Coroner) who know that it happens.

Charles Dickens was a reporter before he became a novelist. He was also an insomniac, who often passed his sleepless nights by walking the beat with London police officers. It was perhaps from one of them that he learned about the deadly fire, for he knew about it and described it in detail in *Bleak House,* giving details that could only have come from someone who had seen such a death.

Charles Fort was an American who devoted his life to collecting accounts of 'anomalous phenomena'. He published four fascinating anthologies of them, *The Book of the Damned* (1919), *New Lands* (1923), *Lo!* (1931) and *Wild Talents* (1932). He died in 1932 and his books are out of print in Britain. There is a collected edition of all four by Dover Books in the United States, and his work carries on here in the pages of *Fortean Times,* a monthly magazine.

Fort knew about spontaneous combustion and cited many cases. He also knew about scientists, and all of his books contain atrociously silly denials and preposterous 'explanations' by scientists of phenomena they did not understand. Maybe all science students should have a compulsory course on Fort's work before entering their profession.

Fort and others have defined certain common characteristics of SHC. The victims are, as Doctor Trotter said, often drunkards. They are frequently, though not always, female and usually of advanced age. The heat destroys most of the body, leaving only odd limbs, and does so without setting light to inflammable substances close nearby. Sometimes victims seemed to have burned inside their clothing, which remains largely unharmed, sometimes even within their own skin. The effect seems to occur almost instantaneously, as the victims are rarely heard to cry out. Frequently, there is no possible source of ignition in the vicinity.

There are, however, cases that do not fit this profile. There are young children, youths, young women and men, even corpses, who are struck by SHC.

In January 1939, 11 month old Peter Seaton was put to bed. Shortly afterwards a visitor to the Seaton home heard the child scream and rushed to the bedroom:

"It seemed as if I had opened the door of a furnace. There was mass of flames that shot out, burning my face and flinging me back across the hall. It was impossible to get Peter out". That staid and unemotional newspaper, the *Daily Telegraph* believed Peter's death was SHC.

Nearer our own time and in our own area, 3 year old Cassandra Wickenden died a similarly dreadful death in Birmingham in 1980. Fire officers and a detective told the inquest that there was no source of ignition in the child's bedroom, but suggested the fire might have started from a cigarette burning in the next room. Her distraught mother shouted, 'Nobody had been up there - it did not start like that.'

Cassie's parents fought to call a psychic expert at the inquest, but Coroner Dr Richard Whittingdon would have none of it, saying 'I do not accept this as evidence in court'. Perhaps he should have done, for Cassandra had a strange history. She was a hyperactive child exhibiting strong psychic talents, causing objects to move at her will. She developed a ghostly playmate, who her parents thought to be imaginary until her father saw him. They called in a Baptist minister to rid the house of Cassie's 'friend', successfully. After a week the little girl noticed his absence and called him back. Coroner Whittingdon recorded an open verdict.

In August 1938, 22 year old Phyllis Newcombe was suddenly covered in blue flame as she danced with her boyfriend at the Shire Hall, Romford. Her partner and others beat at the flames, but 'within minutes' she was 'a blackened mass of ash'. A cigarette or a match brushing her dress was blamed, but her father produced a piece of the dress material at the inquest and showed that it could not be so ignited.

In 1985 Jackie Fitzsimmons, a cookery student, felt heat on her back as she walked down a corridor of Halton College Widnes after a cookery exam. Within seconds she was on fire. She was hospitalised and two days later had recovered from three per cent burns on her buttocks and back to such an extent that she was sitting up and chatting, and made a statement to the police. Two weeks later she relapsed and died.

Manchester's Shirley Institute, the most prestigious independent forensic laboratory in Britain, whose speciality is textiles, was briefed by the Fire Brigade and produced a 30 page proof that Jackie's clothes could not have ignited from accidental contact with a cooker five minutes before the accident. The Coroner did not admit the report as evidence, no fire officer was called and the Coroner warned the Jury to 'ignore all the talk in the media about SHC'. A verdict of misadventure was found.

Mrs Sam Satlow of Oregon died on 7th December 1973. For three days she lay in a closed coffin in the local Chapel of Rest. Early on 10th December she burst into flames and was consumed to the hips. An intensive police investigation found no cause.

Some victims survive. In 1974 American Jack Angel had his right arm burned off by SHC but lived. In 1805, Professor Hamilton of Nashville was walking home on a cold evening when he felt a steady sting in his left calf. Looking down he saw a 6 inch blue flame shooting out of his leg. He cupped his hands around it, depriving it of air, and it vanished. His leg showed a 3/4 inch livid injury. His long winter pants had a tiny hole but his trousers, through which the flame had emerged, were unburnt. They merely had a powdery deposit on the inside.

19 year old Paul Hayes was attacked by SHC in Stepney Green, London, in May 1985.

"It was like being plunged into the heat of a furnace .. my arms felt as though they were being prodded by red hot pokers, from my shoulders to my wrists. My cheeks were red hot, my ears were numb. My chest felt like boiling water had been poured over it. I thought I could hear my brains bubbling ... I tried to run, stupidly thinking I could race ahead of the flames .. I thought I was dying".

Then it stopped. The flames disappeared and there was no smoke. He stumbled to the nearby London hospital where he was treated for severe burns, but his shirt, though scorch marked, was not burned.

Some really bizarre cases involve the deaths of people who were in the act of suicide when SHC took over. In September 1952 Glen B Denney cut his wrists in the kitchen. Then he caught fire. The Coroner decided that, after slitting his wrists, and with arterial blood spouting everywhere, he had gone into his bedroom, soaked himself in paraffin from a non existent (or never discovered) container and set light to himself.

Billy Thomas Peterson sat in his car in Detroit in December 1959 and burned to death. His jeans and underwear were only slightly damaged and the car's full petrol tank did not ignite. Only Peterson, part of his seat and a plastic religious statue on the dashboard burned. Billy had attached a hose to the exhaust and sat waiting for a sleepy death when a more dramatic fate overtook him. The Coroner decided that the carbon monoxide fumes from the exhaust had ignited him. How?

Not all Coroners ignore the obvious. In 1970, Dublin Coroner Doctor P J Bofin (sic) dealt with the death of an 89 year old woman, who was reduced to ashes. He said: "The circumstances of the burning are unusual, and would conform to what is called Spontaneous Combustion".

Until there are more Coroners like Doctor Bofin, and more scientists like Doctor Trotter, deaths like that of Mary Clues will remain a deadly mystery to the public and a huge embarrassment to science.

One last thought. Mary Clues had drunk large quantities of aniseed cordial which was a medicine rather than a drink. A century after her death the expert eater and drinker George Sallas remarked that it was 'much prized in nurseries where the infants suffer from flatulence' and was 'supposed to increase the supply of milk in mothers'. Mary would hardly have been drinking it for the second reason. Sallas also said of it that 'Doubtless it has its virtues, but has a sickly taste and may well be left among the medicine bottles of the nursery'. He did not seem to regard drinking it as an incendiary pastime.

Shropshire

The Room Where Time Moved Back

(Bridgnorth)

From Anglo Saxon times England has been divided into shires, shires being subdivided into 'hundreds' as smaller administrative units. Representatives from the hundreds were partly responsible for law and order, and a 'hundred house' would therefore serve as the local Magistrates' Court.

Robert Creswell bought the Punch Bowl Inn in Bridgnorth, a former hundred house with a licence that went back to 1740. Opposite the Punch Bowl is a former tithe barn, now a house, which still has horse mounting blocks.

"On the first floor is a passageway with bedrooms leading off it. One morning in about 1980 I went to go into the end bedroom and found that I could not open the door. I put my foot against it and forced it open. A small boy who had been playing with a young girl was knocked over by the opening door. Both children were wearing Elizabethan dress. Sitting on a seat in the room were a lady and gentleman in their early 30s. The most noticeable thing about them all was that they were wearing wide, white Elizabethan collars or ruffs, including the children. They took no notice at all of me. Surprised, I glanced round the room and happened to look out of the window. Instead of seeing a road I saw what I deemed to be a cobbled courtyard. The tithe barn was part of the structure of the building.

I stepped back out of the room and closed the door. The next time I went there the room was back to normal".

★

Did Robert Cresswell stray into another time? Was he the ghost or were they the ghosts? Would they later tell their friends about the rattling doorknob and the door that opened of its own accord?

Timeslips are among the rarer paranormal incidents and amongst the most difficult to explain. Some are undoubtedly forms of hallucination, born from what the observer knows of a place or what they have read or imagined, but some are so complete and realistic as to shake that idea. If you believe that time is an endless ruler, running from past to future, and that we progress steadily along it, then timeslips ought to be impossible. Our understanding of the more rarified areas of modern science is pretty weak, but we seem to have grasped the idea that time may not be a straight line. To speculate in our own terms, what if time is like the groove on a gramophone record, a spiral whose loops lie close together? On a ruler, 1998 will be equidistant from 1898 and 2098, widely separated, but in a spiral they may lie close together. Perhaps we sometimes jump, like a gramophone pickup, into an adjacent track. Are there cases (and we cannot know if there are) of people who jump into an adjacent track and cannot return? Thousands of people disappear without trace every year. If people from the past or future do jump into our time, you will probably find them in mental hospitals.

Or perhaps time is a more complicated shape. Perhaps it loops in several dimensions and perhaps there are many places where different times are close together (the timewarps beloved of science fiction writers). Time is, after all, a human concept, a set of rules we have created to convince ourselves that we understand the way that aspect of the universe works, and perhaps we are wrong. After all, we were wrong about the earth being flat or hollow, and the impossibility of heavier than air flight.

Another possible explanation of timeslips is that certain places have the capacity to retain a recorded image of incidents that have taken place there and that some people can trigger a replay of those images. This idea was memorably dramatised in Nigel Kneale's TV play *The Stone Tape*. If this is the case, it would explain not only timeslips, but many historic hauntings and the perplexing re-enactments of battles that are seen or heard in some places. See also *Midland Ghosts & Hauntings* page 124, 'The Phantom Battle' for the Battle of Edge Hill.

The Haunted Engine

(Horsehay)

Horsehay is, in part, a ghost village. A large railway depot once stood here with shunting yard, hoists and offices, together with an enormous factory making giant cranes which could lift an engine. Now the factory has been replaced by a housing estate, and of the railway depot only one shed remains. The train runs on Sundays only and the track, once part of the Severn Valley line linking Kidderminster to Shrewsbury, is now a mere half mile long. It is run by a voluntary trust who are struggling to conserve something of the area's past.

Paul Noakes, a member of the Trust's Committee, told us:

"My older brother and I used to walk past the sheds every day on the way home from primary school and sometimes we would stand and look in. Then the workmen would chat to us and tell us about the ghosts. The last train ran in 1965, and by the time I was at junior school in the late 1960s the place had already become derelict, with rotting boards and broken windows.

My older brother was mad about trains and we used to come poking around. One of our favourite places was a derelict shed with huge sliding doors on the outside. Inside were joists to haul up heavy goods, and offices three stories high still full of old books. We often heard strange noises in there, like a heavy man's footsteps going along the concrete floor. One lovely summer's day we saw, a few yards away, the shadow of a big man appear like a puff of smoke through the wall on the one side of the shed. It went gliding across the platform and disappeared out through the opposite wall. Although it only lasted a few seconds we both saw it. We felt as well as saw it - it was a weird sensation, like a whiff of cold air.

There is still paranormal activity in the Horsehay sheds. Sometimes you put a tool on the line and the next minute it's missing and no one has been near. A lot of it seems to be centred round engine number 5619. It has been said for a long time that you could hear the gears moving when no one was in it".

One bright July Sunday in the 1980s, another member was sitting in the office having a cup of tea.

"I heard footsteps on the opposite side of the locomotive. I called out, 'Hullo, hullo.', and went to see who it was, but no one was there. I went back into the office, and a few minutes later the same thing happened again. I heard it twice within the next hour or two. This happened again a few months later".

One of the older committee members of the Horsehay Trust was the late Bernard Lewis. He said that a lot of people had heard these footsteps and they belonged to one of the old engine drivers who had driven a locomotive in the 1930s. He knew the man and one day had seen him walking down the platform. Bernard spoke to him but the engine driver didn't reply, he vanished straight through the wooden partition at the end of the shed. Bernard said, 'Taint the dead buggers you have to watch out for, tis the live ones'".

No. 5619, an 0-4-2 tank built by the GWR in the 1920s.

Young Paul was a new member of the Trust and had not been warned about the ghost:

"I was working here on my own, having arranged for a friend to come along to help. When I heard the footsteps I thought he had arrived and was amazed to find no one was there. It happened three times. The third time I waited outside the shed for him. When my friend turned up he said, 'What's the matter with you?' I said to him, 'You'll think I'm stupid', and I told him what had happened. He told me that they often heard it. Although it spooked me out the first time, I'm used to it now and it doesn't bother me.

The strange thing was that the engine 5619 was away for eighteen months, and during that time not a single footstep was heard. As soon as the engine came back it started again".

Michael, Site Manager for seven years, says:

"We only hear the footsteps when 5619 is in the shed. This engine was built in 1924 and worked in the South Wales coal fields. When the age of steam came to an end in the early 60s it finished up at the Barry Island scrapyard and was then brought here. As far as I can gather, somewhere in the past it acquired a ghost which has followed it. You can hear his footsteps and you can hear that he's there, I've often said, 'Good morning' to him. One chap was working in the shed one day and he heard someone approach so vividly that he said, 'Pass me the spanner'. When nothing happened he looked round and found no one was there".

Michael's wife has never seen the ghost, but she does have something to say.

"About 1990 I was standing on the platform with our dog, Max, a Staffordshire Bull Terrier who was then 2 or 3 years old. The 56' engine came in and the dog watched it quite calmly. He knew the engine driver so that he didn't bother about him, but suddenly his hackles went up and his tail and ears stood on end. Then his head moved as his eyes followed an invisible something along the platform. The souvenir shop was then inside the shed and the lady in the shop said to me, 'Your dog has just seen Fred.' (that's what we call the ghost). I couldn't see anything".

Former Trust Chairwoman, Wendy, had a much more dramatic experience in August 1995:

"In the middle of the heatwave, I was working on a bench outside the shed. There was brilliant sunshine, it was hot and dry without a breath of wind and no one else was there. Suddenly, I felt a strange sensation - a slight coldness and a feeling of great sadness. A yard or two away from the bench were three large flower pots, and I suddenly noticed that the flowers were being gently pulled forward, one by one. First one pot, then the next, then across to the third, as if someone was walking along sniffing them. I was standing there, shocked more than anything, when a man's voice spoke to me. The words were quite meaningless to me but I will always remember them, they were 'car, grif, thrim'. I rushed out of the station gates to get to my car, but as I went round the corner heard the fire buckets (which are kept just inside the doors) rattling violently, making a great noise. The shed was all locked up and quite empty.

Last Friday, I came to a committee meeting. As I work in the evening I have to join the meeting at about 10.20. It was pitch dark. As soon as I got out of the car I could smell burning and heard a crackling noise as if something was on fire. I looked up and I was horrified to see that the breeze blocks at the top of the building were on fire, with flames flickering out of them. I rushed into the building - nothing. I couldn't believe it. I went outside and looked up and there was no fire, everything was quiet and in darkness.

One afternoon in June 1995 I came out of the crew room. At that time there was an archway at the far end. I looked up and saw the figure of a fireman or driver. He was a youngish man, tall and dark, and he was wearing old fashioned clothes - blue overalls, a loose blue denim coat and a peaked cap like that of a foreman or driver. He had a little bit of black on his face which I thought was very strange, as we were not in steam at the time. He was quite clear except that his face was frizzled, like an old picture, but I could see that he was extremely angry. He walked from the centre of the platform straight out through the door".

★

On an unseasonably warm afternoon in October 1995 we visited Horsehay Trust for the first time. Though the sun shone and the outside temperature was more appropriate to July, the engine shed maintained an icy coldness throughout the heat of the day. We had been there a couple of hours, sitting on the platform inside the shed, drinking tea and talking to Trust members, when we distinctly heard a sound like heavy, booted footsteps, passing along the ridge of the shed roof. We would like to know more about exactly when, and in what circumstances, this sound is heard. If it is not paranormal, it occurs to us that it may be a rhythmic contraction or expansion of the old building's roof structure when the interior lights have been on for a while and warm air from them has risen into the roof.

In September 1996 we spent an entire night in the engine shed and you can read about it in the chapter on ghost watching.

In 1923 all the British railway companies were merged into four groups, the Great Western retaining its name and absorbing the Cambrian Railway and several lines in South Wales such as the Taff Vale. Locomotive 5619 is an 0-4-2T built by the GWR in a batch of 200 engines between 1924 and 1928 to replace the miscellaneous collection of tanks they inherited in this area. We know that this one was allocated to Abercynon shed in 1947, but have not discovered anything in its history which might explain a haunting.

The strange words might well have been Welsh. Our publisher has some knowledge of the language but can make nothing of them, possibly because this is an English rendering.

The Ghost Train
(Wellington)

In November 1963 Reg Stanley was working as a signalman for British Rail at Allscott Beet Factory signalbox, which was on the main line from Wellington to Shrewsbury:

"I was permanently on nights and I was reading a book at about 2 o'clock in the morning, when Upton Magna near Shrewsbury, the next signalbox down the line, signalled one beat on the block bell - the 'Call Attention' signal. I answered with one beat in reply, then he signalled three-one on the block, which meant that a branch line passenger train was approaching.

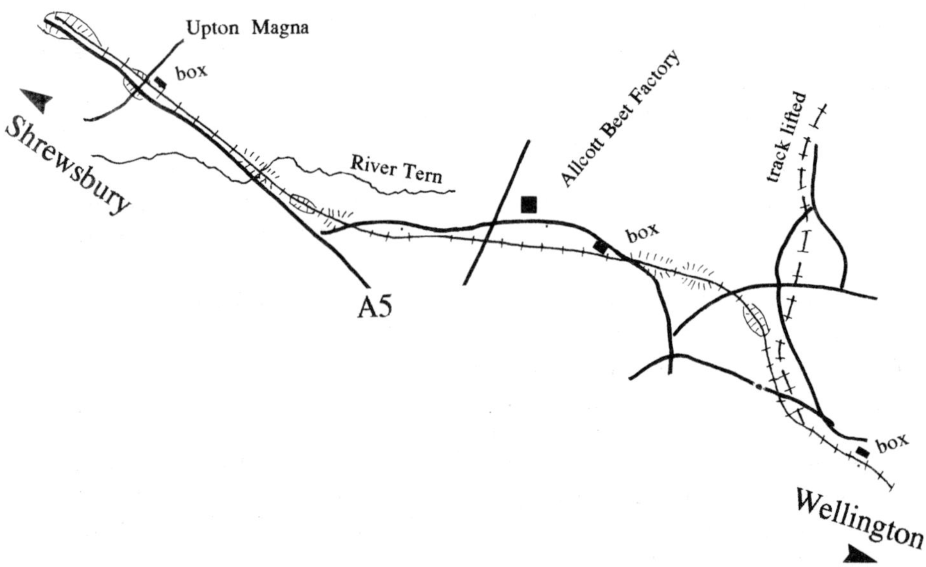

I immediately offered it on to Wellington No 4 signalbox which signalled to say that it had been accepted. I pulled off the signals and then had nothing to do except lean out of the window and watch for the train. It was lit by moonlight and you could see the lights and door handles shining as it went by. It had a Midland side tank engine of the Johnson design, LMS 3F No. 47344, and three coaches. It was a clear moonlit night and I could make out every detail. I could see that there were passengers inside wearing modern clothing. As the train went past it didn't make a sound. I watched the one red tail lamp (which means train complete) and gave two-one beats (Train Out of Section) on the block bell to Upton Magna, and two beats to Wellington No 4 Box (Train Entering Section). When I saw the red tail lamp disappear into the distance I had finished, and was able to sit down and return to my book.

Ten minutes later Wellington phoned me and said, 'Hey, where's that train gone to?' I told them, 'It's gone through here.' They said, 'Nothing has come through here.' They never did get that train and they told me I must have been dreaming and that I was going crackers, but I know what I saw and I know that I wasn't half awake, I hadn't been asleep, I had been reading a book in the signalbox. And I hadn't been drinking. I must admit, it was quite scary.

You have to record all the trains that go past the box in the Train Register book, so I wrote by the side of the entry, 'Ghost Train'. Two days later the District Inspector came to check the register and said, 'What's this?'. I told him what had happened and he said, 'I'll just tick it as read'. There were no more enquiries or anything. So I said no more about the ghost train and have kept it to myself until now".

★

All over Britain there are tales of ghost trains. Is this the only one ever to be officially recorded in British Rail's logs? It would be interesting to know whether any entry appeared in the log of the Upton Magna box.

There was once a branch line between the Beet Factory signalbox and Wellington which headed north to Market Drayton. It was lifted in the 1960s and part of it is now a public footpath and cycleway. However, the branch line's alignment was such that to join it, trains had first to enter Wellington station, so the signalman would have seen it. Of course, if the train was travelling in an earlier time than 1963 when Reg Stanley saw it, then it would have been handled by an earlier inhabitant of the Wellington box.

This type of engine was known as a 'Jinty', a small 0-6-0 tank based on a design of 1899 by S W Johnson, the then Chief Mechanical Engineer of the Midland Railway. This company was merged with others in 1923 to form the Londdon, Midland & Scottish Railway. Number 47344 was one of 422 similar engines built between 1924 and 1931 by the LMS. This identification number was allocated on nationalisation in 1948. If Reg Stanley was seeing something which had occurred in the past it must have been between that date and 1963. Several similar engines have been preserved and one can be seen on the Severn Valley Railway.

Roman Horses
(Telford)

Colin Ayling lives in Telford. His hobby is metal detecting.

"I do not know what happened that night. One person on their own might have imagined it, but when two people simultaneously witness the same event, then there has to be something in it.

John England and I detect on 2,000 acres of land belonging to a country estate. Over the last four years we have built up a very good relationship with the owner and the tenant farmers. The summer and autumn months will sometimes see us detecting all night. We enjoy the peace and quiet, but the night that we decided to search the boulder field was a night we shall never forget.

As we drove out into the countryside on that warm, early autumn evening, there was a strange silence between us. I put it down to a reluctance to want to search all night; but with hindsight, maybe we sensed that all was not well.

Within thirty minutes we had arrived at our destination. It was nice to get out of the car and fill our lungs with good, clean air. The night was warm and balmy, with no breath of wind; ideal conditions for detecting. The prospect of finding that elusive pot of gold had not, however, galvanised us out of our lethargic state. For three quarters of an hour, we just sat on a bale of hay, talking. John heated up two tins of beans while we formulated a plan.

We decided to search the large field directly in front of us. Though it had never produced much in the past, we shared a gut feeling that it had potential.

It was almost midnight as we began our search. Whilst John headed off on his usual, round the perimeter, route, I set off on a diagonal one. Three hours passed before we unexpectedly met again.

All was quiet, except for the occasional clunk as my search head hit a stone. The first half dozen signals produced only iron, but the next produced a coin. Even in the dark I could see the glint of silver as I rubbed it between thumb and forefinger. The profile of an elephant on one side told me that it was a republican denarius of Julius Caesar. Having filled in the hole, I moved on.

Over the next hour I found several Roman bronzes, and another denarius, this time of Rutilious Flaccus. Feeling that my efforts were going to be well rewarded, I resumed my search with vigour.

At that time, I had totally forgotten about John and was quite startled when he suddenly emerged out of the darkness, coughing. 'Hiya Col. Had any joy mate?', he asked. 'Yes, I've had a few coins, Have you had anything?' 'Seven coins and a fibula', came the reply.

All that trudging about had made us weary and we flopped down on a grassy bank at the edge of the field. We gulped down cups of tea and tore at our sandwiches.

We felt rather refreshed as we resumed our search. Working in close proximity, we unearthed four artefacts within the space of forty minutes. Though the items were ancient, we were not able to discern for what purpose they were used. One had the name Nigel punched on its surface, and was obviously a javelin tip. It was then that it happened.

'Col. What's that noise'? 'Sounds like horses,' I replied.

We both stood in silence, as the noise grew louder, and nearer. The ground vibrated beneath our feet as the thundering hooves came straight at us. There were many horses, heading our way.

'Run, John, run!', I shouted. The herd passed between us, as we scattered in opposite directions. Almost as quickly as it had started, the noise died away.

'Col, where are you?', John shouted. 'Over here, mate. Are you alright? Did you see them?' 'No. Did you?' 'I couldn't see anything, but they weren't far away from us'.

We were shaken. Had we fallen under the hooves it could have proved fatal. We just could not understand where the horses had come from. All the fields in that area are arable. Feeling rather unnerved, we headed across the field towards the car. It was then that we saw it.

The field system in that area is well known to us. For almost five years we have searched there. There was no doubt in our minds that we were in a field we called the boulder field because of a pile of boulders in one corner. We had not been on any other field that night, so there was no uncertainty as to our location. Yet, half way across it, we were halted by a very large obstruction.

About 40 metres in front of us was what looked like a hedge. It was about 3 metres tall and very dense, you could not see through it, with a uniform top as if it had been cut. It was brown in colour, with traces of white toward the top. Thinking that we must have strayed in the dark, we walked parallel to it for almost 80 metres. By the time we came to the end of it we were able to look down the slope of the field and see the car. Realising that we were in the right field, we turned around to find that the 'obstruction' had disappeared, causing John to mutter, 'I don't know what has happened here tonight, Col, but whatever it was, it was not natural'. I agreed with him. It had certainly been a very strange experience, one for which we had no explanation.

Walking about in the dark did not appeal to us any more. Knowing that we had not imagined what had happened, we wondered what we had come up against. The safest course of action was to head back to the car and wait for daylight before looking for answers.

While we waited for the dawn to come up, we discussed the night's events. For almost an hour, we walked all over that field in daylight and found nothing, no indication that anything had crossed it during the night. The winter wheat had not yet broken through the surface, and our own footprints showed up, but nothing else.

Baffled, we walked to where we had seen the obstruction. There was no sign of it, but our footprints clearly showed that we had been forced to deviate from our route. From a diagonal course, we had gone off at a tangent for almost 100 metres, before resuming our original course. Something had made us do that.

We were left with only one conclusion. Whatever we had witnessed had been of a supernatural nature. Of that there we had no doubt. For me, that conclusion was confirmed a few weeks later.

On a visit to Shrewsbury we called on Mike Stokes, the archaeologist at Rowley House Museum. He showed great interest in the finds we had made that night, and in their location. There was no recorded evidence of any Roman sites in that particular area. Indeed, nothing had ever been found, even during normal agricultural activity. To say he was delighted would have been an understatement. He was particularly interested in the javelin tip, saying that it was one of the best examples he had ever seen and the only one inscribed in such a personal way. Presumably, Nigel had been a shortened form of Nigelus. For me, the most interest thing that Mike had to say concerned the other finds. They were military bridle fittings, used by Roman cavalry.

We have had a few months now to reflect on the events of that night, but still cannot find a logical answer".

Laying a Ghost?
(Telford)

"It began one Saturday night when my wife asked me if I wanted to go with her to a meeting at the Spiritualist church.

I have been interested in ghosts and the paranormal ever since we were first married. We lived then in an old cottage and had such things as door handles moving up and down and tapping at the front windows. At first we thought that somebody was messing about, but when we leaned out of the upstairs window we could see that nobody was there. Since then we have lived in a number of places, and although we never had any more trouble, I would often get books about the paranormal out of the library.

We had been living in our present house for about two years and my wife had got friendly with a woman who went to Spiritualist meetings. I went with her that night. We had the Lord's Prayer and one or two hymns, then this man went to the front and he started calling one or two people out of the audience and telling them things. Afterwards, my wife asked how I enjoyed it. I said that I found it interesting and I quite believed some of what this man had said.

When we got home we found my son and his girlfriend sitting on the settee, so my wife and I had an armchair each. My wife started taking the mickey out of me, calling out in this funny voice, 'Is there anybody there.' I said, 'Now look, it's my belief, just knock it off, will you?', but she kept on.

At 3.30 the next morning I heard something like a thunderbolt outside the bedroom window. To be more precise, it sounded like an evil growl. It only lasted for a split second, but my wife and I were petrified and we jumped out of bed. Thinking I had better investigate I went into my son's room and said, 'Did you hear that?', but he just turned over and went to sleep.

So, with my wife standing at the top of the stairs I crept down. As I went I felt as if something was down there, on the ground floor. I pushed open the living room door but everything was pitch black. Putting my hand cautiously round the door, I switched on the light and stood back. Something very strange had happened. The TV was face down on the floor and all the pictures had been taken from the walls and laid on the floor. In one case the plug holding a picture had been ripped out.

Everything looked as if it had been set down very carefully. There wasn't a scratch on anything except for slight damage to the paper rack, which I soon glued together again. We put most of the stuff back, but I was so frightened that I hardly slept for the next three nights.

Next day we went back to the medium. She took us to the chapel and put us in touch with another medium, who was a supervisor. He came to our house on the Sunday night and said there was definitely a presence there, and it was very unfriendly. He said that I had brought something back with me from the chapel, and when my wife was taking the mickey it had got angry. He told us not to worry and the disturbances would only last about three months.

At that time I had a little pug dog. I had to get up for work very early each morning, and when the dog saw me he would run into the lounge and sit in front of the fire, whether it was on or not. I was making myself a cup of tea in the kitchen when the dog bolted out of the lounge as if someone had put a boot behind him, and went into its basket in the kitchen. He had never done that before.

Another morning, I had made myself a cup of tea and was about to sit down, when the cat, who had been sitting on the armchair in the lounge, froze, staring at the settee. Then she stiffened and growled. I opened the window and the cat shot out.

Once I was sitting on the settee when I smelt a beautiful perfume, like nothing I have smelt before or since. It was a woman's and only lasted a few minutes.

You could see our house from some distance. One day I was walking home from work and drawing near, when I saw the dark figure of a woman in the window, as if she was waiting for someone to come home. Thinking it was my wife, I waved. She not not wave back, but drifted away as if she was going towards the kitchen. When I got into the house my wife was asleep on the settee.

One evening, I was lying on the settee but definitely not asleep. My wife had gone down to her friend's house a few doors away. The light was low and I had my arm over my eyes. I was wearing a pair of jeans, and suddenly felt something tender and soft down below. I thought, 'What's going on?' What happened next is too embarrassing to tell in detail. I must confess that

I didn't move immediately, but I soon came to my senses and jumped up. I felt all cool down below, as if I had had a good night with a woman. I made myself a cup of tea, then I went to my wife. She said, 'What's the matter?' I said 'Nothing, but do you mind if I join you for a while?' Shortly after this experience my wife saw a programme about this kind of thing on the TV and taped it for me. I said to her, 'I wasn't going to tell you, but that's what happened to me.' She said, 'Never!'.

Lying in bed one night I felt something going up my legs as if they were being massaged. When it got near my lower parts I jumped out of bed.

While my wife was preparing the dinner one afternoon she heard a loud rumbling noise. She went upstairs to investigate and discovered that all my things, my clothes and my toiletries, had been thrown into the bath. Nothing of hers, only mine. Her stuff had stayed where it was.

The three months predicted by the Spitualist had just about come to an end when my wife was working in the kitchen and heard the noise of a window opening and shutting. Whatever it was had gone out. That was the last we saw or heard of it. Soon after that we moved away, not because of the ghost, but because my wife was having problems with her back and we decided to get a bungalow".

We couldn't think of an appropriate illustration for this story, so skipping to the next - here is Avro Lincoln RF398 from Cosford Aerospace Museum. The Lincoln was a development of the wartime Lancaster, and this one is haunted (see page 61).

Staffordshire

Flying Home
(Lichfield)

In about 1992 Mr Billings was working at Lauas Limited who were using hangars on the disused RAF airfield at Lichfield.

"I heard about hanger Number 5 and the fact that the women would not work there after 6 o'clock. The word went round that the spirit of an airman had been seen. Then while I was working on the old pilot's recreation area, I had the feeling that I was not alone.

Shortly afterwards the company closed down, but my interest had been roused. I found out who owned the site and asked if I could stay there overnight.

At that time the control tower was still standing. At 11.30 pm I had just left one of its rooms and gone up to the roof, when I heard footsteps coming up the steps leading from the operations room to the roof. I went back and found nothing. It was then that I heard a woman's voice, which seemed to come from the operations room. She seemed to be talking to an aircraft. I could make out various letters, and the voice said that the runway was clear to land. For a few minutes the control tower seemed to have

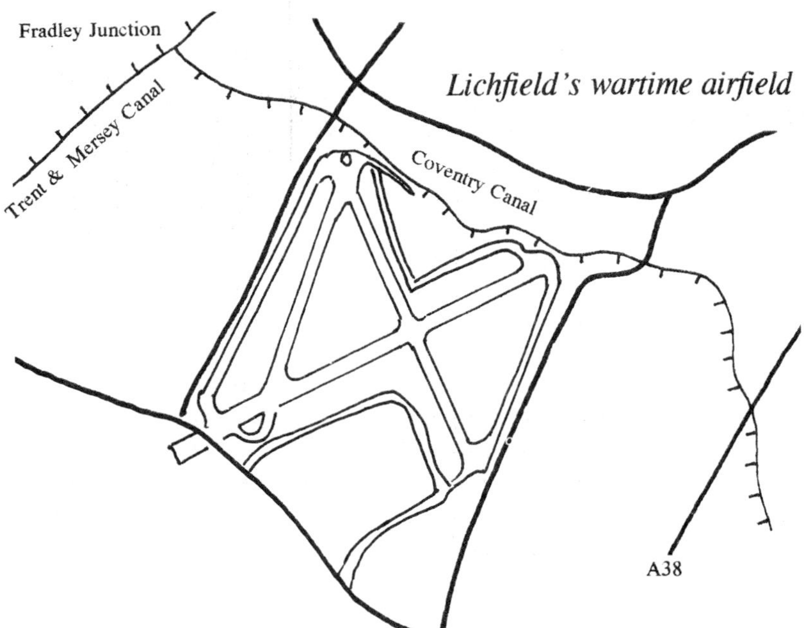

Lichfield's wartime airfield

come alive as it was in World War II. It is hard to explain but I had this feeling that other people were there. This lasted for a few minutes.

Afterwards I went for a walk by torchlight around the runways leading to the main runway. It was then, when I was just about to walk onto the main runway, that I could not move for the terrible wind. The grass was being blown along with me. I can only compare it to standing close to an old World War II propellor aircraft when running its engines ready for take off. Then as suddenly as it started, it was over. The grass was still and I was able to move again. I returned to the control tower and went up on the roof from where I could look out over the airfield.

However, the apparitions had not yet finished with me. At 3.30 in the morning the first rays of daylight could be seen towards Burton on Trent. I was looking towards the canal when I saw a tall young man, I should say in his early 20s, wearing an RAF blue uniform with a yellow Mae West. He seemed to be walking slowly from one of the hangers to the control tower but not getting any closer. The only thing that was strange about him was that I could not see his face. As I watched, he disappeared; one minute he was there and the next he had gone. I went over to where I had seen the figure but nothing was there.

Some weeks later the control tower was pulled down. Maybe the owners had heard of the hauntings and thought that these would stop if they demolished it, but I don't think so, in my opinion the whole airfield was haunted. These young men lived on the base and were flying night after night. Many of them did not come back and Lichfield was the last homely thing that they saw. When you think of the ages of many of these airmen it is hard to believe that they would not return to this place".

★

There seems to be some unexplained connection between fliers and the paranormal, ever since airship days. In *Midland Ghosts & Hauntings* see page 67, 'The Haunted Lincoln', and page 70, 'The Pilot'. The cases of the crew of the R101, the polar airship expedition, the ghost of Flight 401 and many more, imply that airmen are more likely to become ghosts than, say, boilermakers or lawyers. If they are still outnumbered by ghostly nuns and phantom priests it may be only because the religious professions have been around a lot longer.

Old George
(Tamworth)

John Chapman says:

"When I was in my early 20s in the mid 1970s, my girlfriend and I went to the Dog and Doublet in Bodymore Heath near Tamworth. It's a picturesque old pub at the side of the canal. We had a nice normal drink, then returned to the car, which was about 30 feet away from the pub. At that time a privet hedge ran along the bank of the river parallel to the water. The owners of the Dog and Doublet had raised its level so that it was higher than the car park, probably to discourage people from driving into the water.

I like to put the handbrake on and keep the car in gear. We chatted for a while, all the pub lights were out and there were no lights on in the car park so that we were sitting in the dark. All was peace and quiet. It must have been about midnight when suddenly the car shook, moved forward a foot and then moved back.

It dawned on me that anyone who was strong enough to do this to a car was not going to do me much good, so very sheepishly I slowly got out of the car and looked around, but nobody was about. I got back in the car and a minute later, it happened again. The car vibrated violently and moved forward then backwards. I noticed then that there was a full moon, so I could see quite clearly. I had another and more thorough search. I walked all round and even looked under the car. Then it occurred to me that the car park was gravel and no one could have got away without my hearing them. Very puzzled, I got back in the car. Two minutes later the car shook and moved again. This time, I said, 'Sod this, I'm off' and I drove away. The strange thing is that my girlfriend did not make a remark or say anything about it.

I went back to the pub two weeks later and told them about it. The man behind the bar said, 'Oh, that's Old George. He's been here for a couple of hundred years or so. He's quite harmless, he's just telling you to go'.

I returned to the pub last year and discovered that the area has now been grassed over and has benches on it. The nearest I could park to the original spot was about 10 feet away. I sat in the car after the pub had closed and thought that if anything did happen I'd get out of the car and say, 'Hullo!'. Something did happen but it wasn't Old George. The licensee came out at about a quarter to 12 and shooed me off".

★

Was it really Old George, or something else? Later on you will come across another story about a car misbehaving oddly when a couple parked up at night for a snog. Does this happen often? Is it another hazard of courting?

Girls and young women, we know from research into poltergeists, can produce amazing psychic effects and astonishing energy when under sub conscious stress. Is this business of leaping cars some manifestation of a female guilt complex, of not really wanting to do what they're about to do, or even of not wanting to do it with that particular partner. We do not want to discourage young men from pursuing their natural instincts, but have you read Stephen King's *Carrie?*

Does it ever happen to men or women who are alone in their cars? If it does, then we will have to accept Old George or think of a different theory.

Anne in the Fog

(Featherstone)

Anne Kelsall is a legal secretary. In 1982 she lived in Cheslyn Hay and one November evening she decided to go and see some relatives at Oxley, about 7 or 8 miles away, near Wolverhampton.

"The weather was cold and dry, a clear autumn evening. To get to Oxley I had to go through Shareshill towards Featherstone, along the New Road, and then onto the Stafford Road to Oxley.

On the New Road at Featherstone there are very few houses. There is a farm, a permanent caravan site and, of course, Her Majesty's Prison. I had passed the prison gates and was heading towards a junction where there is a garden centre. Between the prison entrance and the garden centre there is nowhere for a vehicle to turn off the road, there being a hedge on each side backed by fields.

I was about 500 yards beyond the prison entrance when, turning a slight bend in the road, I came upon a solid wall of fog. I slowed right down as I approached and drove into it very slowly. It was extremely thick and, at one point, I got very frightened because I could not see a thing and was panicking about how I was going to drive through it.

I stopped the car and wondered about reversing, but it occurred to me that, if someone else drove into the fog, they would surely run into the back of my car. I don't know how long I sat there, probably only a few seconds, but then some lights appeared behind my car. The lights were so bright that I thought they were on a large lorry or van, but they did not blind me in the rear view mirror. They seemed to go 'around' my car.

I looked to the front and found that I could see the road and the gutter at the side. I thought to myself, 'Thank goodness, whoever you are, thank you. I can see to drive through the fog now'. I started the car and drove quite slowly for a distance of about 200 yards until I came out the other side of the fog. I drove a few more yards, then stopped so that I could see who had been my 'saviour'. I wanted to thank them, for the relief I felt at getting out of that fog was tremendous.

I sat waiting, but no one followed me. I got out of the car and listened, but could hear no engine noise. Quite perplexed, I got back in the car and started to drive away. As I did so, I looked in the rear view mirror and noticed that the fog had disappeared.

I arrived at my relative's home and I thought I was OK until I tried to speak to them. I could not get any words out - I was sort of babbling. They could not understand what was the matter with me and I don't know why I could not talk properly, I did not think I had been frightened by what happened, only about not being able to see through the fog. It was about thirty minutes before I could talk sense.

I went home by another route that night, I still don't know why".

★

Nor do we. On the face of it, if there was something paranormal lurking about Featherstone New Road that night it certainly did not mean any harm, but it is surprising how deeply frightened people can be when they come up against things that are right outside their frame of reference.

The Nun on the Bridge
(Alton)

Caroline* is 25. As a girl she attended St John's Catholic Primary School in Alton and recently she and an old schoolfriend went back for a visit.

"Crossing the small bridge from the carpark, we were met by an Irish nun. We explained the purpose of our visit and she sent us in the direction of the Head's office. When we met the Head we mentioned the Irish nun on the bridge. She laughed and said that she, the Head, was the only Irish nun at St.John's, but visitors were quite often greeted by the Irish nun at the bridge."

The Lamp Man
(Upper Tean)

Carol lives with her husband in a modernised cottage up a country lane. About nineteen years ago, when her son, Ian, was 7, she was doing sums with him and talking about comparing people's ages.

"He suddenly asked if his grandfather was older or younger than the 'Lamp Man'.

I said that I didn't know the Lamp Man, so Ian went on to describe an old man that he saw on the stairs. He said that the man had a lamp like old Uncle Bill. Now old Uncle Bill was a miner, and we have his collier's lamp suspended from the shelf over the fireplace.

In the early part of 1978 we had building work carried out on the house. One day one of the builders was left on the site alone to wait for the Building Inspector. When we returned he said that he thought someone had come through the front door, and when he went to look he saw a man on the stairs with an old fashioned miner's lamp.

Later that year Ian produced a drawing. When asked to explain it he said that it was a view of Jackson's shed (Jackson was our dog). The picture showed Ian himself falling over the dog's chain, Pleblings and a Pleb Snapper (who eats Pleblings) and the Lamp Man in the sky. I had invented the Pleblings in the stories I told him. They were little creatures who went about doing good. Ian subsequently invented the Pleb Snapper, that ate them. I still have the drawing and I'll let you have a copy".

★

Which she did, so you can see Ian's drawing of the Lamp Man. We are grateful to Ian and his mother for the story and for permission to reproduce a unique picture.

Why do children see more ghosts than adults? They do, and they are very rarely frightened by them. Perhaps if you can believe in Pleblings and a Pleb Snapper who eats them, it's easy to be undisturbed by a Lamp Man who manifests on your stairs. Young Ian obviously thought that he and his dog, Pleblings, the Pleb Snapper and the Lamp Man were all part of the same world.

A survey about twenty years ago showed that virtually all children are telepathic, but the ability wanes as they approach puberty. Is it a natural feature of childhood that only survives in a few rare adults? Or is it a natural feature of human beings suppressed as children become 'socialised' ie learn to be suspicious and secretive? What little evidence there is suggests the latter and, if that is true, perhaps we are all born with a range of psychic abilities that are repressed by the process of growing up.

Warwickshire

Miss Lucy's Hat

(Charlecote Park)

During the latter part of her life, Alianore Fairfax-Lucy, the aunt of the present Baronet, Sir Edmund, could often be found in the Tack Room at Charlecote Park. She had made it into a comfortable base to which she would walk every day from her home in the Old Malt House in Charlecote.

There was usually a fire burning in the small grate, which is surrounded by the jumble of horse paraphernalia that you would expect in any tack room. The room is dominated by a splendrous array of silver mounted carriage horse tack, whilst from above the mantelpiece a stuffed stag's head surveys the room. It was Miss Lucy's special place and no one would have dared interfere with the arrangements, even when the National Trust opened the tack room to summer visitors.

After Alianore died in 1975, care was taken that the room would retain something of her influence. Some changes were made to prevent people handling or moving items. The Trust built a barrier to allow only a few people into the room at a time, and some furniture was moved out of the way.

In her will, Alianore left the Malt House with all its possess-ions to her nephew Duncan, and before long before he came to live at Charlecote with his family.

The National Trust Administrator at the Park discovered a lot of interesting papers and valuables in one of the drawers in the Tack Room, including Alianore's medical qualification certificates. He invited Duncan to come and have a look.

It soon became clear that the room had been an extension of Alianore's home. In one of the blanket boxes they came across a couple of wide brimmed hats, and were delighted to find that one matched the hat she was wearing in an old photograph of her astride a favourite pony. The photograph was jammed in at an angle on top of the mantelpiece.

Duncan took away the important papers and valuables and the rest were replaced as they were found. They decided to hang the hats on the stag's antlers.

A few days later the Administrator noticed that the hats were missing, and found them back in the blanket box. Realising that he had not told the House Steward and cleaners about the new plans, he replaced the hats on the antlers, making a mental note to speak to the House Steward next morning. When the two men met they went together to the room, through two locked doors, to find the hats were back in the box. It was just possible that one of the cleaners had been moving things, so both men devised a scheme with the keys to ensure that no one else could possibly enter the room and that they could only enter together.

Before they left the room the hats were returned to the antlers, then the doors were locked. The next day both men entered apprehensively, knowing that the hats would be back in the box. They were, and it was only then that the Administrator noticed that the photograph had disappeared. Alianore did not approve.

The Phantom Cat
(Copt Heath)

Copt Heath lies a mile south west of Solihull. A hundred years ago there was little more than a windmill and a Hall, but at the turn of the century there was some residential development in the grounds of the Hall, and Ted Hughes* lives in one of these houses. In 1987 he took a week off from work to supervise enlarging of the house, adding extra bedrooms and a bathroom.

"A few days after the alterations were completed we began to hear footsteps, usually going into the old back bedroom. Doors were open and shut and items were moved. The keys were taken out of the door and dropped onto the telephone table. We also heard bumps and bangs. 'It' seemed to object to my working on the house; whenever I got my tools out there was the most dreadful hammering echoing through the walls.

I do shift work and so I sometimes go to bed early. One summer evening I was in the house alone and in bed, going off to sleep, when I felt the cat jump on the bed and walk about. I told him to lie down and, for a minute he was still, then he started walking round the bed again. Again I told him to stop it. This happened several times until I got fed up and sat up in bed, intending to push the cat away. There was no cat there, but I could still feel something settling down then getting up and walking over the bedclothes. As I watched I could see indentations appear on the bedspread, as if an invisible something were walking over my bed. I said to myself, 'You're over tired.' so I lay down and went to sleep. When I mentioned the incident to my wife, she said that the same thing had happened to her and it had lasted for as long as half an hour.

One weekend I went away and my wife slept in the spare bedroom. During the night she was woken up by approaching footsteps, and felt something standing next to her bed which she could hear breathing. I decided that enough was enough, and something had to be done, so I went to see the local Vicar.

He was a very nice chap and said he would come round and do a blessing. What amazed me was that when he had finished, it went very hot, a blast of hot air went through the house. We have not had any problems since. The Vicar has even done a follow up and contacted us to find out if the haunting had vanished. I think he was quite chuffed that he had managed it."

★

Building operations often seem to disturb, reawaken or even give rise to manifestations in a building. The simple answer is, of course, that the building work may introduce some physical feature that creates disturbance, like poor plumbing or wiring or draughts. Alternatively, changing the positions of doors, windows and walls may simply make evident what could not be perceived before. Yet again, if it is true that some locations have imprinted in them 'recordings' of past events, disturbance by builders may accidentally trigger replays.

Sometimes ghosts disappear after building disturbance. One well reported Birmingham ghost has not been seen or felt for two years since the parquet flooring of its usual haunt was relaid. Then again, was there some fault in the old floor that gave rise to reports of a ghost? Has the new floor prevented some effect of heat or damp or draught, or whatever sparked the stories?

Whatever you do, don't discuss ghosts with your builder, that will lead to walkouts, mysterious illnesses on the job, delays and added expense.

Lady on a Bicycle
(Coughton)

The Throckmorton family acquired the Coughton Estate in 1409 and still live at Coughton Court. This stately structure was started in the early 16th century and its dominant feature, the gatehouse, was completed in 1509. It stands some 200 yards back from the A435, which is the old Roman road, Ryknield Street.

This story comes from Les Parret* and his son, Norman.

"I came out of the army in about 1949 and, together with my son, went to visit my wife's mother at Bidford on Avon. Our return journey from Bidford took us along the A435. The night was very dark and my Austin 7's headlamps were not throwing much light. Just as we came level with the short road which runs down the side of Coughton Court to a ford, a woman on a push bike loomed up from nowhere and I ran over her. There was no bump, nothing. I said to my son, 'Did you see what I saw?' He said, 'Yes dad, you've just run over a lady in a white mac'.

I stopped the car and walked back, but I could see nothing. Opposite Coughton Court on the main road is a row of cottages. A door opened and an elderly man asked what the matter was. I said that I had just run over somebody. He said, 'Had she got a white mac on?' When I said that she had, he said, 'Take no notice of that mate, there's dozens of them run over her.' It turned out that a lot of drivers had seen the same thing.

★

This is another 'vanishing victim'; see also the story of that name under Birmingham.

The Girl in White
(Kenilworth Castle)

Don Horsley was a Supervisor for British Gas. He recounts an experience which had such an effect that he still remembers the exact date - 12th November 1985.

"I went with two chaps to do some work near Kenilworth Castle. One of the men said, 'Let's go down to the pub at lunch time for half a pint', so off we went to the Queen & Castle. We sat in the lounge, a little room which faces the castle, and I sat facing the window. I could see a not particularly exotic part of the building, just a high wall with a dip in it. Through this dip you can see into the castle grounds, which are all lawns with a few sturdy trees dotted about and a steep bank halfway back running parallel to the wall. The day was cold and clear.

All of a sudden I saw a girl aged 16 to 18 walking very slowly across the lawns from right to left, towards the gatehouse. She had long black hair halfway down her back, she was very slim and wore a long white dress which went down to the ground. The dress trailed behind her just a little, not a long train like a wedding gown. Her hands were held out in front of her and placed on them was a big, white book. She was obviously reading it, and because it was heavy she was walking very slowly. At this stage it did not dawn on me that there was anything odd about her, but then she went behind one of the trees and never came out the other side, and the tree was only thin.

I said to my mates, 'I think I have just seen a ghost'. They said, 'You what?' I told them, 'You'll have to excuse me, I'll go and check it out'. I went to the man on the gatehouse and told him what I had just seen. Then I nipped up the driveway and looked all round. There were several people about but it was much too cold to be wandering round in a white dress, and they were all wearing gloves, scarves, anoraks. It was quite obvious the white lady was not there. I returned to the man at the gatehouse and described the girl to him. He said that he had not seen anybody like that.

When I went back to the Queen & Castle everybody said, "Ah, how much has he had to drink.' I said that I had been in the pub only 4 or 5 minutes and taken only a sip or two of my half pint.

About a fortnight later I was at a house in Kenilworth when the owner had a visitor. She mentioned that she lived by the castle, so of course I told her about my experience. She said that about three weeks previously the local paper had a feature about the ghost and a picture. Later, I went to the paper's offices. I felt a right twit, saying that I had seen the Kenilworth ghost. The editor showed me the piece, which told how a lady went out to a musical event with the WI. As she was sitting listening in a room with a big crowd of other women, an apparition suddenly appeared. She was the only one to see it. She told the newspaper who used a model to act as a mock up of the ghost. When I saw the photograph of the mock up I said to the editor, 'There's only one thing wrong, this girl is wearing a flowered dress whereas the ghost was wearing a white one'. The editor said, 'I know, we told her to put on a plain dress but she turned up in one with flowers on it'".

The view into Kenilworth Castle from the Queen & Castle pub is currently blocked by building work, but this is the lawn which Don would have seen.

The Mickleton Hooter

(Mickleton)

Meon Hill was a supposed to be a witches' meeting place. At its eastern foot is the small village of Mickleton, famous for a curious phenomenon - the Mickleton Hooter. The sound comes from Weeping Hollow, a nearby shrub filled pit with a pool at the bottom. One tale says that the Hooter is the lowing of the ghostly Dun Cow which was killed by Guy of Warwick, a Dark Age thug who liked to slay people. We rather like the sound of the Cow, an enormous beast that shambled round mid Warwickshire causing all the folk who clapped eyes on it to be doomed. The most tragic legend is that a large house once stood near the edge of Weeping Hollow whose owner was a keen huntsman. One day, his young son went to join him and announced his arrival by blowing on his horn, but his father thought he was an animal and shot him with his bow and arrow. Ever since the lad has been wandering around blowing his horn.

The Mickleton Hooter has been put on record many times, including an article in the local paper in 1962 which was followed by letters from two readers who said that they had heard the Hooter. The early '60s were the years of scooter [sic] mania and a scooter club, based in Evesham, decided to visit Weeping Hollow at midnight. The club leaders were Alys and Charles Whiting, and Alys describes the evening's events:

"Late one November evening we went with food and a barbecue to keep everyone entertained until midnight. I can't tell you how eerie it was when we arrived at Weeping Hollow. The night was pitch black with a strong wind so that all the trees and branches were moving as if they were alive. Nervously we parked our scooters, set up some lighting and began work on the barbecue. As midnight approached the conversation died away. Suddenly, the wind dropped and everything went quiet and still. We had a lad with us named Jimmy whose father had a pub at Cropthorne. He had brought a hunting horn and said, 'I'm going to give the Hooter a mating call' and he sounded three long blasts. For half a minute there was complete silence, then up from the darkness of the hollow we heard three long cries. It was the strangest sound, human yet not human, as if it was somehow disembodied.

Everyone snatched at their equipment and was away. We were bringing up the rear and had to wait until last.

One just possible explanation of the Hooter is that a pair of bitterns have set up home in Mickleton. Their cry has been described as a booming sound and is said to resemble something between a lowing cow and a distant foghorn. Bitterns normally nest in the fens but have lately been recorded on some of the wetlands in Warwickshire, such as Kingsbury Water Park and Brandon Marsh. However there would be precious little suitable habitat at Mickleton, and the long life of the legend would require generations of bitterns. It is must be the dreaded Cow.

The Grey Nun

(Princethorpe)

Helen Staff has told her story many times and has not yet found anyone who believes it, although she says that she knows without any doubt that it is true.

"In 1938/9 my father bought an acre of land at Burnthurst near Princethorpe. He had a bungalow built and moved in when he married in June 1939. The land backed onto Princethorpe Great Wood and behind that was a Priory and convent school. Every fine Sunday, the nuns in their black habits would take the girls out for a walk, which took them past my father's bungalow.

My mother was sitting in the house one day in the early 1950s when she saw a nun in a grey habit (the Priory nuns wore black) walking up the front path. Mother went to the front door and opened it but found no one there. She glanced back and saw the nun passing the bay window and walking towards the back door. She rushed through the house to the back door and opened it, but there was no one there either. At this point I arrived home from school to find my mother standing outside the house, looking puzzled.

This strange phenomenon occurred several times over the years, always in the summer and always at approximately 4.30 pm."

Readers might care to look at another story about the same area called 'The Nun, the Priest and the Redcoats' on page 119 of *Midland Ghosts & Hauntings*. It mentions that the convent and school were built in 1832 for a group of French nuns who had fled their country during the revolution. After staying at a number of places they found a permanent home at Princethorpe.

Nuns are Britain's favourite ghosts, seen in hordes all over the country. One would imagine that after a lifetime of self denial, prayers and hard work, they would go straight to heaven when they died, but an alarming number of them seem to haunt the earth. They are closely followed, numerically speaking, by 'grey ladies' who may be out of focus nuns.

It is not quite clear whether this case is a nun or a grey lady. Not all nuns wore (or wear) black habits, Dominicans and some Franciscans wear white or cream. However, the nuns at Princethorpe Priory wore black, and this ghost wears grey. Perhaps she is not a nun. Maybe she is simply a lady in a long grey dress with an old fashioned head dress that looks like a wimple.

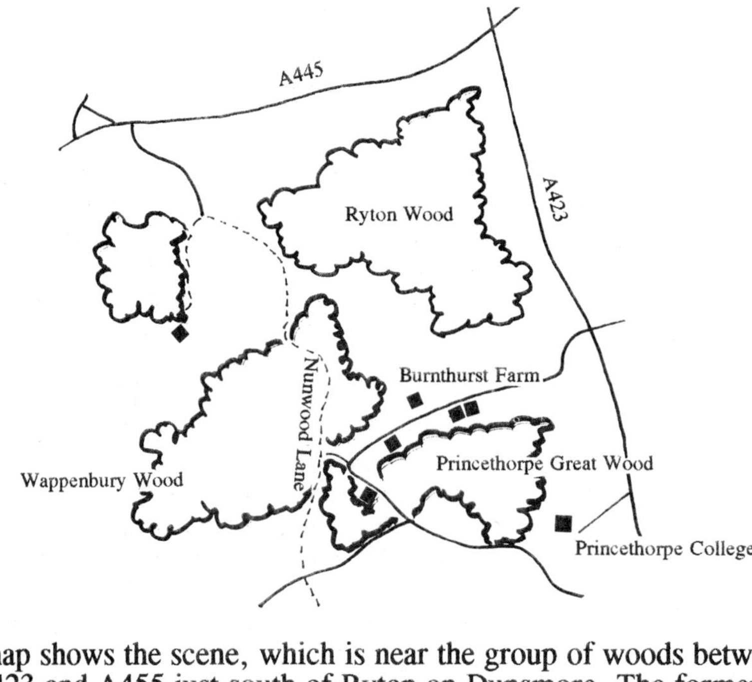

Our map shows the scene, which is near the group of woods between the A423 and A455 just south of Ryton on Dunsmore. The former school and Priory are now Princethorpe College, an independent Roman Catholic school which nevertheless accepts children of all denominations. Like most Catholic foundations in Britain, the Priory was established only in the last century when sufficient religious toleration existed. We wondered if the local names of Nunswood and Nuns Wood Lane were associated with an earlier foundation (which would have been closed down by Henry VIII at the Reformation) but we have found no evidence of one.

Long Boney Fingers
(Quinton)

Lower Quinton was very much a small country village until the housing shortage of the early 1950s, when it was enlarged by housing estates. In one of these new houses lived Linda Cox*, together with her parents, two brothers and four sisters.

"We were a very happy family and very close and protective. I was the youngest and I slept with my sisters in one bedroom; it was in here that most of the strange events took place. We did wonder if it was haunted. My mother told us not to be silly, but she slept there once in later years and during that night she had a frightening experience of something holding her down.

Sometimes I put things down but they were gone the next minute; the question was, had I mislaid them or had been been spirited away? Once I bought a brand new red and white striped T-shirt, took it out of the bag and the next minute it had disappeared. I never found it

I remember waking early one morning to find myself lying on my back and feeling that I could not get up. I managed to move my hand and felt, lying next to me, an icy cold hand with long boney fingers. I lay there not daring to move. That was a horrible experience. Although at the time the feeling was very real, when I looked back I wondered if I had a bad dream. I could not prove that I was awake.

However, there are two events in my life which I am certain were not dreams and not my imagination. Both took place in my bedroom at Quinton. One was a minor incident but quite strange. My second eldest sister was first in the family to marry when she was about 20 and I was about 15. I woke up in the night to hear this pure, clear heartbeat echoing off the walls. It was incredibly loud. I am certain this was not a dream because I know that my sister heard the noise, too. She whispered to me, 'Are you wide awake, Lin?'. I said to her, 'Can you hear that noise?' and we lay in bed, discussing it and wondering what it could be.

The most frightening incident occurred when my eldest sister was about 18 and I was 7 or 8. I woke up in the middle of the night to see a woman standing on my sister's bed, about halfway down, where my sister's chest would be. The woman had long grey hair in a plait and an old fashioned, dark Paisley pinny with a bib. Although it was dark, I could see the pattern on her pinafore, which somehow seemed to give off its own light. She was bending down looking at my sister with one hand on her hip, and with the other she seemed to be scratching her head. I was terrified. I know this was not a dream because I kept shutting my eyes tightly and opening them, hoping that the woman had gone, but she was still there. I wanted to get off to sleep but I was so frightened that I couldn't. I watched the dawn break and when it got light, she disappeared.

When I described the figure to my mother, she said it sounded exactly like the woman who had looked after my sister when she was small. My sister said that she saw her quite often, but for her the woman did not disappear with the daylight".

The Feel of a Cat

(Studley)

Ghostly animals are not all that uncommon. One of the more famous examples is the white horse of Tysoe which has been seen, this century, by a local lay preacher, a postman, a policeman and in 1947, by soldiers based in Burton Dassett. (See *Midland Ghosts & Hauntings).* A housewife who lived in High Street, Studley, between 1980 and 1987 reports that she had a ghostly cat.

"I wasn't the only one to feel it, I have four children and each one of them felt it. At night, as soon as you snuggled down into bed, you would feel the cat jump on your bed and turn about, but when you put your hand out nothing would be there. It would come and curl up, not on the edge of the bed, but right up next to your legs. Then it would shift around, as cats do. It would settle on the bed quite regularly and we would feel it about once a month, perhaps more often. We knew it was a cat because the children could sometimes hear it purring.

The first couple of times we were rather apprehensive but after that, we just expected it. The children still talk about it".

Jenny Burntail & the Luminous Owls

(Avon Dassett)

Mysterious lights that float across the countryside at night are seen in many places and known by a variety of names, such as 'Will o'the Wisp' or 'Jack o'Lantern'. In Warwickshire they are called 'Jenny Burntails'.

Warwickshire's Jenny made her most famous appearance at a time of political paranoia in Britain. Reports of strange lights and of engines heard in the sky were coming from all over the country. Popular rumour attributed them to airborne spies. Alternatively, they were Soviet aircraft secretly delivering weapons to British revolutionaries. This was in the wake of the bitter and protracted coal strike of 1921.

In the little settlement of Burton Dassett a Jenny Burntail was seen, and swarms of reporters descended on the area to spend cold February nights lurking in fields. They recorded seeing a light, 'as bright as a car headlight', that sometimes floated, sometimes darted about, and sometimes just hung about in the branches of trees.

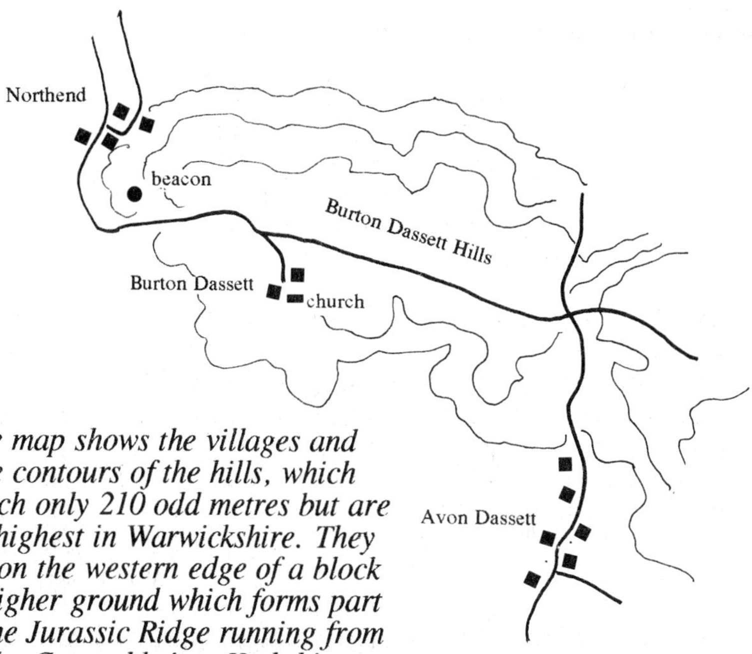

The map shows the villages and the contours of the hills, which reach only 210 odd metres but are the highest in Warwickshire. They are on the western edge of a block of higher ground which forms part of the Jurassic Ridge running from the Cotswolds into Yorkshire.

No one could explain the phenomenon until one expert declared the cause to be a 'luminous owl'.

Now we would love to believe in luminous owls, but we are assured that there is no such creature. It belongs in that bizarre bestiary from which 'experts' derive their 'explanations' when faced with unusual phenomena. One recalls the highly polished ducks, whose bellies reflected streetlights so brightly that a team of academics from an American university thought they had photographed a UFO; or the very mathematical hedge hogs of Wiltshire that mate in perfect circles, thereby causing crop circles. Then there was the blue, whirring bird that lived in Queensland thirty years ago and was mistaken by locals for a flying saucer; the whirling crocodiles which mated in perfect circles in the lagoons of northern Australia and caused crop circles in the reeds.

So, if it was not a luminous owl keeping the reporters amused in 1922, what was it? Well, a recent incident in the same area may offer an explanation. A housewife from the next village of Avon Dassett told us:

"One Monday lunchtime in the spring of 1989, I had a most curious experience. I remember that it was a clear, frosty day, and it must have been Half Term or Easter because my son was at home.

At about 2 o'clock I heard the crows making a terrific noise outside my back door, so I went out and looked up. I have seen crows scaring away owls and buzzards many a time, but I have never before seen them behave like this. There were about a thousand of them, all circling above our house, not horizontally but obliquely round and round and making a dreadful racket.

I went back into the house and called my son to come and see. As I turned back to look up again, the crows parted and I saw an object, around the size of a football, hanging in the sky. It was very slightly elliptical and looked as if it were made of stainless steel. I saw it for two or three seconds before it moved sideways so rapidly that it was difficult to follow, and disappeared over the side of the hill.

I often wonder if this was in any way connected with the ball of light that was seen repeatedly at Burton Dassett during the 1920s and was said to manifest itself from the side of the church."

Now it might be thought that this lady saw a mechanical device, but if she did, in that same area where something was seen in the 1920s, it would be an extraordinary coincidence. There would be no reason why a flying machine that was hovering over Warwickshire in the 1920s should still be around (or have come back) 65 years later. What is more, had it been mechanical it is unlikely that it would have caused such an unholy disturbance among the crows. Most British wildlife has long learned to live alongside man and his machines without panicking.

If it was not a flying machine, what can it have been? Our reporter's description of the thing is, happily, very precise. She carefully states that it looked as it were made of stainless steel, not that it was made of it. Was it, perhaps, something that was not as solid as steel, but shone enough to create a metallic appearance in daylight? Was it, in fact, something that might have shone brightly enough in the dark to be a Jenny Burntail?

What kind of object shines brightly enough in the dark to be mistaken for a headlight, shines sufficiently in daylight to be taken for polished steel, moves about fast and erratically, hovers, reappears in one place for some time, vanishes for decades and seriously upsets birds?

There is such a phenomenon. The movement of underground rock formations creates electromagnetic 'blobs' that discharge into the atmosphere above ground. They appear only when the right kind of rocks are moving, they glow in the dark, they hover and dart about and they shine in daylight. What is more, if one passed through a flock of crows, its electromagnetic aura would disturb the magnetic areas of the birds' brains. 'Geomagnetic lights' as they are called, are now believed by many investigators to be the source of many UFO reports.

Not perhaps as romantic an explanation as a Jenny Burntail or an ancient spy plane, let alone a luminous owl, but one that seems to make sense. Avon and Burton Dassett lie under the southern flank of the Burton Dassett Hills, which are an outlier of the Jurassic Ridge and therefore oolitic limestone. However, we have not looked further into the geology of the area. If our theory is wrong we fully expect to hear from those who have.

The White Lady of the Springs
(Alcester)

In *Midland Ghosts & Hauntings* we told the story of the apparition at the Springs on the A435 by Ragley Hall. About halfway between the entrance and exit gates of the Hall at the side of the road is an old stone horse trough fed through an iron pipe by a spring.

At the beginning of this century it was said that an elderly lady would be seen standing there, begging a lift to Dunnington cross roads from any passing vehicle, only to disappear before reaching her destination. She became such a nuisance that the owner of Ragley Hall - Lord Hertford, was asked to do something about it. He arranged for the ground round the Springs to be excavated and there they found the bones of an elderly woman, which were interred in consecrated ground.

We believed that this manifestation of the world's most famous and widely travelled ghost, the Phantom Hitch hiker, had been laid to rest, but though she seems to have given up begging rides some of the time, people have continued to see an apparition of a white lady at the Springs right up to the present.

Pat Horton comes from an Alcester family and her mother saw the apparition as long ago as 1912.

"Before mother was married, she used to go dancing on Saturday nights at the Three Horse Shoes. A crowd of about ten young local girls used to go all together, then after an evening spent dancing they would walk home along the A435. Near the Springs are a series of marks in the bank, as if someone has been trying to make some steps, known locally as Jacob's Ladder. One night in 1912 at about 11 o'clock as they approached Jacob's Ladder, they saw a misty white lady floating across the road from left to right. They all shouted and ran. None of them had had anything to drink."

Bob Butler says,

"My dad told me stories of the White Lady of the Springs more than 30 years ago. Then when I was about 17 I was in the Nelson and a man came in who had passed through Arrow on his way to Bidford, and he was speechless. He said that he had just seen the ghost of a white lady cross the road by the Springs. We had to believe him because he was so white; he couldn't hold a drink."

Gordon Spires is dead, but his sister says that his party piece was a tale about the night that he saw the white lady at Ragley Springs. In 1950 he was 18 or 19 and in the Royal Air Force, stationed at Evesham. Each time he was on leave he had to make his way home across country from Evesham to Alcester, which was particularly difficult when his leave started at the end of the day. Once, he managed to hitch a lift as far as Wixford, but then had to walk the couple of miles home. He was passing Ragley Springs at 2 or 3 o'clock in the morning when he saw the White Lady. He took to his heels and ran.

Anne Cooke describes a more recent sighting:

"On Valentine's Day 1995 my husband came in late from work. I rushed to greet him but saw immediately that something was wrong. He looked white and shaken, and his first action was to walk round the house putting all the lights on.

We live in Redditch but both work shifts in Exhall, so that we drive along the A435 nearly every day and at all times. My husband had been on his way home at about 10.40 in the evening when his headlights picked out a white shape in the trees just by the Springs. As he drew nearer he looked more carefully and saw that it was a young lady wearing a white dress, crouching high up on a branch of the tree. Suddenly, to his horror, the young lady jumped off the tree and was left hanging by her neck. It was a grisly scene and it really shook him. He slowed down and looked back but the woman and the tree had disappeared.

On Wednesday 10th January 1996 between 7 and 8 in the evening, my husband was driving past the same spot and again saw some kind of apparition. This time it was a grey shadow set back about 4 feet from the road, standing with arm outstretched. The next day it was my turn to drive along the A435 so that I was roughly in the same place at the same time. I could not believe my eyes as I approached the Springs. There was the same apparition that my husband had described, in the same spot. It was a very ragged figure, grey and misty, so that you couldn't tell whether it was male or female. It was just standing there with an arm outstretched.

I had the children in the car so I just drove past at speed. I was trying to tell myself that it was a reflection or something, but there was no mistaking what it was".

Worcestershire

Chasing the Bear

(Redditch)

Vernon Hopcraft is a retired engineer whose relatives lived at 8, Bates Hill, Redditch, from 1932 until the house was demolished during the development of the town.

"Forty years ago this was a busy little community. The large Apollo warehouse now occupies the site of Bates Hill Wesleyan Chapel, opened in 1843, with cottages crammed back to back on the hill below. The Chapel was on a raised site, so that when the retaining wall round the graveyard crumbled, the residents of 8 Bates Hill found themselves staring out of their back bedroom windows at tiers of coffins which had been buried one on top of the other.

No.8 was once two cottages, but when I knew it they had been converted into one and the building was a general store leased to my grandparents. It had two bay windows with the shop door in between. My grandparents lived with their eldest grand daughter. Several years later, just before the Second World War, they were joined by their youngest daughter Elsie Dillon, her husband Jack and their three children. Elsie and Jack were music hall artistes and usually on tour.

My grandmother never mentioned the hauntings to people, as she thought this could be detrimental to business. She used to hear footsteps going up the stairs and around her bedroom, and every night before going to bed, she would wedge a big pair of scissors under the latch of her bedroom door because on occasions the latch would lift. Her eldest grand daughter was also aware of night time footsteps and a presence in her bedroom at the back of the house. As a child she would ask what she thought was her grandfather for a drink of water, which of course she didn't get. Not only was her bedroom door shut each night, but the only access to the stairs was through the closed door of the rear parlour. The outside door would be locked as well.

During the war Elsie and Jack had to give up the stage and they took over the running of the shop, while my grandparents moved on to open another shop in the town.

When my cousin was a teenager, she and her mother were sitting reading one evening in the living room at the rear of the house. My cousin heard a voice say,

"Open the door." She got up and opened it and her mother asked, "Why did you do that?" My cousin replied,
"I heard a voice ask me to." At the same time her father was walking home down Bates Hill. He entered the house through the front door, using his key and asked his wife and daughter,
"Who was that who's just gone out of the front door?". They said they hadn't had any visitors, and he said,
"Well, someone has just walked out and down the hill."

Their eldest son was a very steady character, intelligent and despite his short stature, very strong. When he was 18 and home on leave from the army, he had gone to bed, having earlier heard the footsteps along the landing. He was lying on his stomach on the bed reading a book, when whatever it was put hands on the back of his neck and held his head down into the pillow. As he told me the story afterwards, he said that it required considerable effort to shake it off. He was terrified, though this is the only time when it has attacked anyone.

His parents were not the type to be unduly worried by the supernatural and both believed that it was harmless.

During the War, my aunt and uncle entertained servicemen who were convalescing in Bromsgrove Hospital. One evening my aunt was chatting to a patient named Clarke and discovered that he had been raised in 8 Bates Hill prior to the 1930s. *(The Needle District Almanac* [the town directory] shows one J L Clarke at the address from 1923 to 1932.) When she told him that she now lived there, he said 'You've experienced the ghost then.' Obviously the existence of the Bates Hill ghost was well known.

The manifestations were not confined to No 8. A lady I knew worked for many years in a small factory opposite. It was several storeys high with wooden stairs to the upper floors, and she told me that something used to walk up the stairs to the top of the landing. She would open the door to see who was there but there would be no one.

In 1995 I worked with a man called Peter Bourne who was one of a large family from Adelaide Street which was connected to Bates Hill. He told me that many times he and his friends, when children, had chased a figure they called 'the brown bear' along a passageway between the houses in Bates Hill and a parallel row which fronted on to William Street. At the end of this passageway was the tall brick retaining wall of Bates Hill Wesleyan Chapel and here the 'brown bear' would disappear.

In 1948 I was courting my wife who lived on the other side of Bates Hill. One bitterly cold night we had arranged to meet at 7 pm. Being early, I walked down Bates Hill hoping to meet her coming up. As I passed number 8 I noticed, toddling along in front of me, a little old person, bent over, wearing a long draped overcoat. I was walking the faster of the two, and gradually closed the distance between us. We crossed the road at the junction of Adelaide Street and continued along the raised pavement on the right hand side of Hewell Road. I was still getting closer when suddenly I realised that the figure was no longer in front. On the right hand side of the pavement were 6 foot high corrugated railings, and on the left, fencing with a drop down to the roadway. A young, agile person might have negotiated the side next to the roadway but the aged person that I was following would have had some difficulty. However, I looked over the railings just in case but no one was there. I wondered afterwards if I had seen 'the brown bear'.

In 1984, during site work for building the Apollo warehouse, a quantity of unknown bones were excavated. They were taken to Bromsgrove Hospital for a Coroner's report and reintered at the Abbey Cemetery on 25 January 1985".

The Vanishing Customer
(Redditch)

Halfway down Bates Hill, Redditch, is a specialist bicycle shop. It is kept by Lenny Rudge, who says that weird things happen every day.

"Our main problem is with the shop door. It needs to be pushed quite hard to be opened. Sometimes people think we are closed because they push it gently and it doesn't budge. Yet time and time again I find the door open when I know that I left it closed. The other day I rushed up the hill to get a bag of chips. You can see our shop from the fish and chip shop, and I was watching it all the time to make sure that no customers went in. Halfway down the hill with my chips I noticed that the door was open.

I came into the shop saying 'Can I help you?' - but there was nobody there. I thought someone had gone into my workshop, but there was no one there either.

We had a rep who came into the shop last winter who said that he didn't believe in ghosts. While he was in the workshop we heard the door open, but when I went out into the shop it was empty. I called to the rep, 'Quick, come in here and look.' He was amazed when he saw that no one was in the shop., He said, 'But I heard the door open.' I asked him whether he now believed in ghosts".

The Curse of Dagnall End Farm
(Beoley)

"It is not so long ago that old Charlie Forster of Dagnall End Farm used to walk his cows down the B4101 at Beoley to reach fields on the other side. The farm belonged to Charlie's uncle, Fred Forster, who later sold off 150 acres which were developed into a golf course. Charlie went to help his uncle in 1935 or 36 and stayed on for nearly sixty years. When Uncle Fred died the farm went first to his wife but then to Charlie. Charlie was the last of that line of the Forsters when he died in 1992 at 78.

Charlie was a local man and we had been friends since my early teens. He was a real countryman, very forthright but astute and knowledgeable. Towards the end he was very ill and I would go up to the farm every night to look after him. I used to be a real disbeliever, but I saw something there that made me change my mind. Each night I used to park in the farmhouse courtyard then walk round to the back of the house which they used as a main entrance. One spring evening in 1992 I opened the gate, got back in the car and drove through, switched the headlamps off and got out of the car. It was then that I saw the dark shape of a tallish man at the gate. He startled me because he had not shown up in the light of the headlamps. I said 'Hullo' but he didn't reply, he just stood by the gate as if he was going to come through. I moved towards the gate but he had gone. I did not think that it was quite the right time to mention this to Charlie - to a sick man, alone in a house lit only by paraffin lamps, late at night. But I did tell him a day or two later and that's when I heard all about the ghost of Dagnall End Farm

Back in the 1850s when the Forsters first had the farm, they took in a Reuben Bennett to work for them. Bennett used to enjoy fishing. Between the back of the cow barn and the neighbouring property was a small river stocked with trout. Uncle Fred owned an acre of land on the other side of the brook, so Bennett used to fish from there, which had a better vantage point. Now, Bennett was having a liaison with a servant girl who worked for the people who owned Beoley Paper Mill and they used to meet at the Village Inn, Beoley, at Holt End. She became pregnant but he was not in a position to do the right thing and marry her. It's not so far to walk from Beoley Paper Mill to Dagnall End Farm, so the people from the Paper Mill kept coming over to Dagnall End. They gave Bennett so much stick that in the end he hanged himself in the big barn, which is just inside and slightly to the left of the main gate.

According to Charlie, this apparition had been making a nuisance of itself for some years, with irregular but frequent visits. An important feature of the apparition was that it was carrying a fishing rod, although it didn't have one when I saw it. It only showed itself in the evening and it used to come from the back of the barn, through the gate (where I saw it) into the courtyard. Then it went round the courtyard and round another building to the stream, where it would sit in Bennett's favourite spot on the other side of the stream, fishing.

What worried Charlie was that the family at the Paper Mill had put a curse on Dagnall End Farm for 200 years. The Forsters had suffered various mishaps, no one from the family had done much good and indeed, the line ended with Charlie. He was worried that if the ghost had manifested itself, might not also the curse? Was the ghost there to make sure that the curse was implemented? Could the ghost fulfil the curse by becoming malevolent?

I remembered then how Charlie used to barricade the back of his house; winter and summer it was all barricaded shut. The windows were heavily barred and at the first sign of the sun going down, the shutters were up. Now I knew what Charlie was afraid of, it was not night visitors from this world but from the dark world beyond".

★

In 1875 James Haywood, a 40 year old farm labourer, appeared at Warwick Assizes charged with the murder of 80 year old Anne Tennant. A press report called it a 'singular case, and said that one third of the villagers of Long Compton, where the murder occurred, believed in witchcraft. Haywood had killed the old woman with a pitchfork because he believed she was a witch, and justified himself by quoting Leviticus, 'A man also or a woman that hath a familiar spirit, or that is a wizard, should be put to death'. The Judge was appalled by the case and said that 'such a prevalence of this superstition would be disgraceful to savages'. Although Haywood was admitted to be sane in all other ways, he was found guilty but insane.

What would that learned Judge think if he knew that one of the writers of this book is regularly consulted by people who believe that they have been cursed, or that someone has put the 'evil eye' on them, or is ill wishing them?

In the last few years of the 20th century it is astonishing how many people believe in curses, city dwellers as much as elderly country people. In fact, curses only work if you do believe in them. Probably the most famous cursing ritual in the world is the Australian Aborigines 'pointing the bone', which definitely does bring about sickness, mental disturbance and sometimes death in its victims. However, it works only when they know that the ritual has been used against them and when they have a powerful subconscious belief in its efficacy.

That is not to say that you can protect yourself from being cursed by going around announcing that you don't believe in all that rubbish. If your subconscious still believes in it, you will merely make yourself a more helpless victim. If you really think you've been cursed, find someone who understands the way these things are done and ask them to take it off you. That works.

Anyway, the farm and its buildings have now been converted into several private dwellings, while the curse may have moved over the road because the golf course has gone and more of this once blissful rural area has been partly developed.

The Girl at the Cross Roads

(Crabbs Cross)

At the Crabbs Cross traffic island, three miles south of Redditch, roads to Stratford, Evesham, Bromsgrove, Redditch and Birmingham converge. Richard Churchley was driving round here shortly before midnight when - but he tells his own story.

"A hobby of mine is folk music, and the autumn of 1982 saw me driving back home to Astwood Bank after an evening at Bromsgrove Folk Club. I had to come up Windmill Drive hill and go round the island to take the last exit. As I got level with the corner where there is a hedge backed by some trees, I saw this strange figure.

It was a most beautiful young woman; she was like no one I have seen before or since. She had long golden hair, an attractive face and there was a kind of golden aura about her. I can't remember what clothes she was wearing, it was hair and face which stand out most clearly in my memory. There was the feeling of an angel. Her one arm was sticking out and she had her thumb in the air, but she wasn't moving at all, she was just stationary. I only saw her for a matter of seconds as I drove past. I felt that there was something weird about her so I didn't stop.

I'm not offering any explanation, in fact it could have been a real person because these halogen lamps do throw an orange glow, but she certainly looked most unearthly and I must say that the time was ten minutes to midnight. It is unusual for a young girl to be hitching a lift at that time of night".

★

We have already met the world's best known and most widely travelled ghost hanging about the Springs by Ragley Hall, but you should not be surprised to see the Phantom Hitch Hiker anywhere. It occurred in our last book, *Midland Ghosts & Hauntings,* where we added a few pages of comment.

He/she has been reported all over Britain, right across America, all through Europe, in Russia and the Far East, so a couple of different places in the same region will be no problem at all. It is only surprising that Arthur Dent and Zaphod Beeblebrox do not seem to have met him or her in their travels around the galaxy.

Sometimes the Phantom Hitch Hiker is an ordinary seeming man or woman, but sometimes appears as an angel. The angel version usually offers a prediction about the future of the driver or the world, before vanishing. In 1960s America, the angel hitch hiker was transmuted into a radiantly beautiful hippy in white clothes with long golden hair and beard who made predictions.

It sounds as if Richard came across the angelic version, maybe waiting at a five way junction to see in which direction she would be carried next.

More seriously, the persistence of the Hitch Hiker in so many countries and cultures has become a subject of academic study, notably by Professor Jan Harald Brunvand in America who has devoted two books to the phenomenon. A number of roads in Britain are particularly associated with the ghost, for example, Blue Bell Hill in Kent and a road near Frome in Somerset.

The Hitch Hiker is usually seen (and picked up, rather than left standing at a roundabout) by professional drivers, and one has to wonder whether or not it is a hallucination emanating from the minds of bored, tired, drivers who are sub consciously wishing for company or for something to happen.

Richard does not fit that category, but then - he did not pick her up. As to his musical interest, there is now at least one song about the Hitch Hiker - *Laura - Strange Things Happen,* and another about a real hitch hiker who is given a ride by a phantom truck driver.

Magic Boards

(Great Witley & Feckenham)

Gavin lives near Great Witley;

"In the 1980s ouija boards were very popular and my friends and I were always holding seances. We would make our own board, writing all the letters and numbers on bits of paper and arranging them in a circle on mum's best polished table. All the lights would be off except for a small table lamp. Our parents didn't mind us playing this game as it kept us quiet for the whole evening and saved on electricity.

This one night I persuaded my aunt and uncle, both total sceptics, to join me in a game. My mum, dad and sister were also playing. The old tumbler was moving away, spelling out the answers to the usual questions such as age, profession, where did he die etc. Then suddenly, the lights went on in the house and there were several loud bangs in the farmyard outside. There was another almighty bang and the door to the room flew open. My uncle went berserk and insisted that he and my aunt went home straight away. He hasn't spoken to me since."

Jim Frost is a retired engineer and a very sensible, practical individual.

"Although my bungalow is modern, the site is very old and was once a clearing on the edge of Feckenham Forest. A row of cottages stood here which have now been completely demolished. I am told that they included a forge and that they were only tiny, but highly populated, with about twenty people living in one of them.

One morning in 1993 I was woken at about 1 o'clock by something which went straight across in front of my vision. Instantly I was wide awake, and I saw, clear as anything, the head of a Victorian woman. This head was very distinct and quite solid, although it was without colour, just black and white. The woman was oldish, I would say about 60, and I say Victorian because she had old fashioned ringlets. She was looking at me with a very sweet smile. She was there for a few seconds, then just faded. The next day I spoke to my very nice neighbours and told them that I had seen a ghost during the night. The wife said, 'Do you know, we were playing with a Ouji board last night and we frightened ourselves to death.'"

The planchette (French - little board) is sometimes used instead of a glass on a Ouija boad. A wheeled platform with a clamp to hold a pencil or pointer, it can also be used on blank paper to produce automatic writing. The version shown was made in about 1920. It came with a sheet marked not only with letters and numbers, but also days and month, and useful answers to questions such as 'Do not risk it', 'A dark man', 'In three weeks' and so on.

★

The ouija board (not ouji or weegee) is merely a device for releasing the subconscious of those around the table. It has long been established that the 'mysterious' forces that drive the glass or the planchette are the muscular spasms of the extended arms reaching out to the glass.

You can ignore horror tales about people becoming demonically possessed through playing with ouija boards and there is no reason whatsoever to be frightened of them. Most of what appears in ouija sessions is rubbish and even when it seems to make sense, it does not stand up to analysis. It is also a device with which even an amateur can fake results.

This is not to say that you will never get a meaningful message from a ouija board. If there is someone in the circle who is a psychic you may get predictions, messages for people at the table or elsewhere. Even so, most of the time spent at the ouija board is wasted.

There are a few simple rules about the ouija board. If you are seriously interested in the paranormal, don't waste your time on it unless you have a psychic to sit in the group. If the ouija board frightens or disturbs you, leave it alone. If somebody tells you that you can become possessed by using a ouija board, recommend them to a good psychiatrist.

The noisy and sometimes destructive physical effects that are sometimes produced are similar to poltergeists, on which we have already commented under 'Stephanie gets Things Moving'.

The Jumping Car
(Finstall)

We came across a jumping car in Staffordshire, but it appears that they are not confined to that county.

"In about 1975 I had a boyfriend who liked to end our evenings in a handy layby having a cuddle. One evening we went to a dance and decided to return home along the Bromsgrove Highway which had only just been completed. I was driving and he said to me, 'Pull in at this layby', which was the one nearly opposite the Finstall turning.

I pulled in, switched off the engine and turned off the lights. Everything was silent, then I heard a car engine running. At first I thought it was a car driving past, so I waited and was quite surprised when nothing appeared. I realised that it was my own car engine, which had mysteriously restarted itself. I carefully switched off and once more everything was silent, but again the engine started running, and this time I was conscious of a definite throbbing or vibration in the car. I now felt quite scared and said to my boyfriend, 'I'm not stopping here any more, I'm going home.' I switched on the lights and to my amazement, found I was parked on the central reservation. During those few minutes I had somehow moved sideways from the layby to the middle of the road. A car came past and seeing me parked there, the driver pulled up and asked if I needed any help. He thought I had had an accident".

Dark Figure in the Night
(Stourbridge)

Bob Drinkwater describes himself as an innocent youth of 15 in 1941:

"I had been working at Robert White's Tailor and Outfitter in Stourbridge for about six months. Most of the Stourbridge folk of around that time will remember the shop, which sold good quality suits (both ready made and made to measure) shirts, ties, underwear and with a good stock of hats and caps. It was demolished years ago to make way for Barclays Bank.

Behind the shop and standing on its own was a large, empty house, the old Skelding residence, part of which still stands today. Elts the Photographers had recently moved out. The rooms had high ceilings and there was very little light filtering in through the grimy windows. Dust lay everywhere. It was a forbidding place and I detested having to go into that building at any time. Unfortunately there were no toilet facilities in our shop, so every time Bob White or myself wished to answer the call of nature we had to use a connecting door at the back of the shop, enter the old house and make our way to the loo on the first floor.

The war was on and air raids were pretty frequent. Bob White and myself took turns to fire watch at the shop. One murky evening in November, I bade Mr White goodnight as it was his duty that night.

There were no air raid alarms during the night and I cycled to work to open the shop at 9 am. Mr White usually left for home at about 7 am. I approached the front door, key in hand, but to my surprise found the door was open. Bob White was still there, in a highly nervous and excitable state. I asked him why, and I now set down exactly what he told me.

'I came in as usual last night at about half past 9. I made the bed up and then read the paper for some time. It was a pretty quiet night with nothing doing at all. At about half 11 I turned down the gas fire, got into bed and fell asleep quickly.

At about 2.30 in the morning, something disturbed me. I woke with a start, switched on the bedside light, held my breath and listened. I was half expecting to hear bombs dropping in the distance, but there was dead silence. I had reached out for my pipe when I saw it - a tall figure dressed in black at the bottom end of the shop. It came towards me and passed round the back of the camp bed. I sat up and said, 'Bloody hell, what's that!' As I turned I saw the figure disappear through the closed back door'.

He told me that he lay awake for the rest of the night wondering if his visitor would return, but he was left in peace.

Many times afterwards Bob White recounted his eerie tale to callers at the shop. I did have slight misgivings about the truth of Bob's experience, but these were dispelled by Ted Boucher from next door. He said, 'You remember Elts the Photographers? Over the last few years three girls were employed there as assistants and each one of them swore that they had seen a dark figure on the stairs, dressed in black, and they were terrified of being left alone in the old house'.

Mr White had two daughters, both very charming girls, and should they read this I am sure they will remember the story of the ghost".

The Great Hound of Worcester
(Tinker's Cross)

Tinkers Cross is a country road junction just west of Worcester. Victorian antiquarian, Jabez Allies, wrote in 1856:

> "There is a cross road called Tinker's Cross in this parish, where formerly stood an old yew tree, said to mark the site of a criminal's grave. This place is said to be haunted; and Mr John Presdee of Worcester said that one night about fifty years ago one of his father's servants came home to Millham, in Alfrick, frightened almost to death, and stated that he had been to see his father, who lived in Gallows Lane, in Leigh, and as he passed Tinker's Cross on his return home, he saw a strange thing there something like a lion, with eyes as big as saucers. Mr Presdee said that the man appeared to be perfectly sober at the time and that he was ill for several days afterwards, from the fright".

This could be just a quaint Victorian ghost story, but what about the following two incidents? Lower Broadheath is about 2 miles from Tinker's Cross.

"In 1990 when I was 13 I was very friendly with our next door neighbour, Nick, who had taken me under his wing. Late one evening he asked me if I would like to go with him to fetch a Chinese take away from Worcester. It was a dreadful night, with a dense white fog and sleet. Nick was driving very slowly, peering into the fog, and I was in the front passenger seat. We were travelling away from Worcester on the B4204 and had just reached the bend by Lower Broadheath when suddenly this enormous, white, snarling dog leapt on to the bonnet of the car. It was like something out of a nightmare. Another car was coming in the opposite direction but Nick was driving so slowly he was able to stop immediately. I hate to think what would have happened had he been going any faster. I shut my eyes for a few seconds and when I opened them again the apparition, or whatever it was, had disappeared. Afterwards my knees were shaking like jelly".

The second incident is from Tenbury Wells, about 14 miles north-west of Tinker's Cross.

"I was parked up in Poke Lane in Tenbury, in 1968. I know exactly when it was because I can remember which girl I was with in which car, it was my old green Mini. We were in a farm gateway and we were listening to an account on the radio of the Russians invading Czechoslovakia. The lane is supposed to be haunted; poke is an old word for spirits. Suddenly, a really ferocious jet black dog jumped on the bonnet. It was like something out of a horror film, foaming at the mouth and baring its fangs.

I slammed into reverse, whizzed the car round and shot down-hill. At the bottom of the hill I stopped, took a breath and said, 'Shit! What was that?' Suddenly, the great animal leapt onto the bonnet again. I could not believe it. Nothing could have gone down the hill at the speed we went. I took off again and this time I didn't stop until I had delivered my companion safely to her home".

Whispering in the Wind
(Sambourne)

Dr Ray Shaw lives in Sambourne, a village some 4 miles south of Redditch. He is a scientist who worked in the nuclear industry industry for nearly 20 years and moved there in 1991.

"When the government cancelled my project I had the spare time to investigate a phenomenon. This had been puzzling me almost from the time that I moved into my house, which is one of a small group of former farm worker's cottages between two very old half timbered farm houses about half a mile from Sambourne village green.

I am a light sleeper and since we have been in the house, I have regularly heard the vague sound of human voices singing or chanting at about 4.30 am.

For a couple of years I paid this no attention, thinking that the milkman had parked his float outside with the radio or cassette player turned down low. The sounds are muffled and indistinct as if shut in somewhere. As the noise only lasts for about 10 minutes, I was quite sure that it was the milkman.

One thing puzzled me. The sounds have rhythm and cadence with what appears to be a lead singer followed by a chant of several voices repeated over and over again. To call it musical would be rather flattering, but it does sound vaguely like an old English folk song. I certainly was not going to get out of bed on a cold morning and ask the milkman. However, when we stopped having milk delivered the sounds continued.

Then I thought that it might be my neighbour's radio, but the noises continued when he went away on holiday.

We came here from the Lake District where the frequent high winds cause singing in the phone wires. If this was the cause, why is it only heard for a few minutes at 4.30 am? Being a lot more interested now, I soon realised that I still heard the noise when there was no wind at all.

I tried to locate where the noise was coming from. Opening a window had no effect, the noise was just 'around'. It may sound silly, but it was almost as if the house was acting as a receiver.

I began to try improbable theories like removing the bedside radio, thinking that it might function even when switched off. No effect.

Military aircraft regularly fly over the house during the day. I had a vague recollection that houses situated near powerful radar beams can suffer odd effects. Could a radar guidance system be turned on and tested at 4.30 am? My son, who is a qualified pilot, buried that theory by saying that modern military aircraft use satellite guidance systems.

I told my friends about the sound and they nicknamed it, 'The Chanting Monks of Sambourne'. I admit that I did look at local maps to see if there was any evidence of monks being in the area. All I could find was Studley Priory, and although I thought that it would make a good story, I did not think I could convince anybody that ghostly monks from Studley were making a special journey to haunt me.

When I told my story in a local pub it turned out that it was village history that Dominican Blackfriars had taught at St Joseph's RC School in Sambourne, and they were reputed to have walked round the village in single file with their cowls up.

Mediaeval clocks were developed so that monks everywhere could hold services at the same time. All my scientific restraint was now going. I began to wonder whether my house was some sort of telephone exchange through which both living and spectral monks held services at 4.30 am.

I thought that this rather mad idea was finished when I heard the noise at 5.30 am. This puzzled me and then I twigged. The clocks had gone forward one hour and the noise took no account of British Summer Time which was introduced in 1916.

I had heard about Ley lines where a large number of places of worship appear in a line. Some people think Ley lines have magical significance, others that they are lines of electromagnetic energy.

I got some Ordnance Survey Landranger maps which show churches, Roman forts, ancient sites, cairns etc. I started to play around with a ruler but soon found it easier to use a piece of cotton and blutack to mark out straight lines through my house. I found nothing of significance associated with St Joseph's but was astonished when I found an almost straight alignment of eighteen churches between Beaudesert (Henley in Arden) and Worcester which included my house. These churches are Beaudesert, Henley, Morton Bagot, Studley, Feckenham, Bradley Green, Himbleton, Tibberton, Warndon, ending up with the nine churches in the centre of Worcester.

As a scientist, I began choosing places on the map at random and putting dots in fields to see whether I could get similar results. I could never get more than two churches in line with the place chosen. The alignment of eighteen churches was extraordinary. I did some very simple calculations to see whether the line could have arisen by chance. It has the same probability of arising by chance as any one person winning the Lottery jackpot ten times. The alignment was deliberate. But why?

Using maps, I began tracking the line east and west and ended up at Caldey Island in Carmarthen Bay in the west, and Little Walsingham in north-west Norfolk in the east. I noticed an extraordinary number of ruined Abbeys, ancient forts etc on the line. I decided that I would come back to them later.

I can say with total honesty that I did not know the significance of Caldey Island or Little Walsingham at the time. I had to look it up in books.

At Little Walsingham in 1061, the Virgin Mary appeared in dreams to Richeldis de Faverches, the lady of the manor, and told her to build a replica of the Holy House at Nazareth where the Archangel Gabriel had told Mary that she was to be the mother of Christ. After a series of miracles, this was done and Little Walsingham became a major destination for pilgrims. Pilgrim's Ways led there along lines of churches.

Caldey Island is known as the 'Isle of Monks' and there have been four monastic settlements there. There are a great many prehistoric remains, showing that the island has been a place of worship since prehistoric times. I am convinced that there is some sort of connection between Caldey and Walsingham.

There is a church at Marden in Herefordshire on the line and a nearby stone fort - Sutton Walls. The church stands on the site where Offa, King of Mercia, had Ethelbert, King of the Angles, beheaded in 794. The line also goes through Offa's Dyke.

Pope Gregory the Great wrote a famous letter to St Augustine, the first Archbishop of Canterbury, in the late 6th Century, instructing him to build his churches on sites of pagan worship. Why? But as sites of pagan worship were built in lines we are back to Ley lines and the extraordinary line of churches from Beaudesert to Worcester.

I don't think that I am psychic but I do feel that I am being led somewhere. Whenever I want information, it seems that books containing what I want almost fall off the library shelf and open at the right page. My house is marked on the map as 'Sambourne Reins'. I went to Alcester library. Literally the first book that I found was a 'Dictionary of English Place Names'. 'Raines' at the time of the Domesday Book (1086) meant 'shelter, hill or knoll'. Since the ground is flat, it probably was 'a shelter' but for whom?

My thoughts went back to the chanting. Pilgrims would follow the shortest route. The line of churches points towards Little Walsingham and I originally thought that it was a Pilgrim's Way, and that churches were 'mile posts' through the very dense forests of Feckenham and Arden, but is it possible that the line is, first and foremost, a Ley line and pilgrims would be drawn to walk down that and that the line of churches simply indicates the direction of the Ley line?

En route, mediaeval pilgrims slept in a variety of places. If they couldn't get proper accommodation, they slept in barns or under a hedge. Two very old farms which probably stand on a site of even older barns, and a name which in Old English means 'a shelter'. Too much of a coincidence?

A natural question from sceptics is, 'Has anybody else heard this noise?' My wife has heard a noise, but is not too keen to talk about it and says that it is 'singing in the wires', or a radio being played a long way away. She has never heard the noise in the morning, only late at night. She describes it as a faint whining going up and down, drifting over the fields. When she tries to concentrate and listen the noise just fades away. She has heard it several times and thinks that it occurs about midnight. I have never heard that noise.

With the conclusions that I was coming to, I decided to try and find out at what times mediaeval monks held services. The most important time as far as we are concerned is Lauds which is held at sunrise, and Matins which used to be sung or recited at mid-night. Matins are now joined with Lauds and are not sung at midnight. I don't need to elaborate on the disappearance of the midnight Matins in connection with the noises that my wife hears at that time.

I was chatting casually in a pub to an Irish woman who asked 'Do you know what Ley lines are? One goes through Tom's Town and across the Park to St Mary's Church'. However, it kinked around the church and not through it. 'My' line goes about 50 or 59 yards right of the church.

I only set out to try to explain a noise I could not understand and in no time at all I am in the midst of Ley lines, shrines, druids, monks, pilgrims, ancient temples, psychics, books which practically open themselves at the right page, thoughts which just pop into my head when I can't find a piece of information and, overall a feeling that I haven't really started."

★

Well, Dr Shaw is certainly right when he says that all his scientific restraint had gone. It is always nice when a profess-ional scientist approaches the paranormal with an open mind, but it's a shame if he does not apply the same methods that he would in his profession.

Has anyone thought of recording the sounds and digitally 'cleaning them up' so that they can be amplified and maybe identified? Why not use directional microphones, to determine exactly where the sounds begin and end? Why not set up sound operated still or video cameras to see if anything is visible when the sounds occur?

Ley lines? The man who first used the term was Alfred Watkins, a brewer's representative in Herefordshire in the 1920s. Riding about the country, he developed a theory that Britain was crisscrossed with a network of straight line tracks, along which could still be found marker stones, nicks in ridges, pools, copses and buildings. He did not believe that what he christened 'ley lines' were mysterious lines of psychic energy. He believed that they were a forgotten network of tracks and he called his book *The Old Straight Track* (Methuen & Co 1925, Garnstone Press 1970,1972). Four decades later, John Michell published *The View Over Atlantis* (Sago Press 1969, Garnstone Press 1972, Abacus 1973), in which he mentioned Watkins and discussed feng shui (the Chinese belief in sacred 'paths of the dragon') and the work of some UFO researchers who believed that UFOs travel along straight lines, great circles or lines of the earth's magnetic field.

Suddenly, people who had not understood Watkins or Michell started playing with a theory that ley lines were a network of some mysterious energy and that they connected ancient sites. Well, we do not want to denigrate Dr Shaw's attempts to prove that the alignments he has discovered cannot be accidental, but other people have tried looking for alignments of public telephone boxes on Landranger maps and found lots of them. In fact, one mathematician proved that all the telephone boxes in his area lay on a logarithmic spiral.

Dr Shaw discusses a difference of 50 or 59 yards in an alignment, but a thread laid on a Landranger map may cover an area as much as 50 yards wide - a fairly significant possible error in a straight line running from West Wales to East Anglia. As to lines that run across Offa's Dyke - the Dyke is 149 miles long and any line running west from anywhere in the Midlands will cross it. Not much of a coincidence.

There is no doubt that monks did make long pilgrimages to holy shrines, and Walsingham was (and has become again) one of these. But is there any proof that they travelled from Caldey to Walsingham? If they did, would it not have been more sensible to travel by sea? Travelling any distance in Britain during the Middle Ages was a weary, filthy, business if you went by land. Anyone who could travel by water did so.

If Dr Shaw wants to pursue an interest in ley lines, that is entirely his affair, but if he wants to explain his mysterious sounds we suspect that ley lines will not help. His morning sounds occur at dawn and take no account of British Summer Time. Birds and animals, wild and domesticated, wake at dawn and ignore BST, and farm animals are shut in during the night so that their dawn sounds might be muffled.

As to books which open at the right page, anyone who has ever researched anything knows that serendipitous moment when the right information just falls into your hand. Some people call it the 'Library Angel' effect. Pope Gregory's letter to Augustine is no great mystery. Augustine had difficulties with both Celtic Christians and pagans in Britain (at Cerne in Dorset they threw old fish at him) and Gregory was simply giving an early example of the wellknown business technique - 'If you can't beat 'em - take 'em over.'

A Dark Hooded Cloak

(Tardebigge)

At Tardebigge Tunnel the Worcester & Birmingham Canal dives under the A448 Bromsgrove - Redditch road. After 568 yards boats emerge at the Old Wharf near Broad Green. By the bridge is a cluster of old houses and a short driveway leading to Lee Shaw's bungalow.

"Our bungalow is at the end of the towpath near to the tunnel portal. The towpath does not run through, and years ago this is where horses were unhitched from the boats to be lead over the hill to the far end.

This incident took place at 7 o'clock on a Sunday evening in the winter of, I think, 1982. We had just returned from visiting friends. Although it was dark, the area was well lit by the lights of the car and from the houses. At that time we had four dogs and they went in front, followed by the cat, followed by my wife, who unlocked and went indoors.

I was reversing the car back into our drive when I noticed a female figure standing by the corner of the old cottage, which was on my right. She was wearing a long, dark, hooded cloak which reached almost to the ground. At first I thought it was my neighbour from the house who sometimes goes down to her boat in a dressing gown (but without a hood). I put up my hand to wave, then waited for her to cross my drive into her house. Instead the figure walked on towards the old cottage. Later I realised that she could not be going to visit the cottage because it was occupied by an elderly person who always locks up and secures by about 4 o'clock in the winter. When I got out of my car I expected to see something of the woman, but no one was there and I could see 50 yards in either direction. Had she entered my neighbour's house I would have heard her feet crunching on the gravel. It is deathly quiet here at that time of night.

It did not occur to me immediately what the woman was, but I realised when I walked into the house. A couple of weeks later I was speaking to my neighbours. The wife swore that on one occasion she had been walking up from the stable and she looked up to see someone. A second later they had gone.

About six months ago I was parking the car again and thought I saw someone standing by the gate. I just saw it out of the corner of my eye, but when I looked properly there was no one there.

Some time later my wife was speaking to her father about the apparition and he said that the figure of a woman has been seen many times at Tardebigge Top Lock. Local people say that a legger - one of the men who propelled boats through tunnels by lying down and walking along the wall, was killed in the tunnel. He fell off and went under the boat. They reckon that the ghost is his wife who comes looking for him.

North (above) and south portals, and the summer scene at Old Wharf.

Running a Ghost Watch

First, let us get the terminology right - this section is about ghost watches. It is not about 'ghost hunting' and very definitely not about 'ghost busting'. The first seems to mean hunting about until you find a ghost. We can give you no advice about that because we haven't the least idea how you would go about it, let alone why. The second appears to mean destroying ghosts. We are not interested in that, either. We are interested in going to where there are said to be ghosts or paranormal phenomena and trying to find out what happens there. That is what we call ghost watching.

Let us warn you that ghosts do not appear to order. There may be three hundred years of tradition which says that the spectre of Lady Ermintrude walks the Long Gallery every night at midnight, but that is not a guarantee that she will perform while you are watching. Start out by expecting nothing out of the ordinary and you will not be disappointed.

What is the reason for ghost watching? Well, if it is properly and conscientiously done, any result obtained (including negative ones) adds a little to our knowledge of the paranormal. Each watch is like a cross between trying to record a rare creature in its habitat and carrying out an experiment based on a totally untried theory.

If all this sounds very serious, that is only because it is, but it does not mean that ghost watching is not enjoyable. If you organise your watch properly and do it in congenial company, it can be an interesting social event as well as a useful experiment.

So how do you go about it? First, as the shade of Mrs Beeton might say, find your ghost. In other words, find a location with a reputation for some kind of paranormal disturbance. Britain is the most haunted territory in the world, so it ought to be easy, but it isn't. Of course there are historic buildings with well known ghosts in the area, but they are not necessarily the best place to start. If they are open to the public the owners may have difficulty in allowing you in, and if not, they may not want you. Premises on which you might hold your watch fall into three broad categories - private, commercial or publicly owned. There are difficulties about all three.

Private owners often feel that a ghost watch will attract unwelcome attention. Commercial premises may have difficulties over permitting access out of working hours, or again, may fear that publicity will drive away nervous customers. Publicly owned premises may be managed by a bureaucrat whose creed is never to do anything which has not been done before. Do not be disheartened by refusals; somewhere in your area there is a building whose owners will let you in. Keep on asking. The ghost watch reports in this book deal with a local authority owned building, a place of commercial entertainment and a shed owned by a private trust, all of whose owners were extremely helpful once they understood the needs of our group.

Any kind of owner may refuse if they believe that you want to hold an overnight bottle party in their building, at which everyone will get drunk and end up snoring or fornicating in sleeping bags. Make sure that your approach to likely prospects is polite and serious. Do not be surprised if some ask for payment, they may have to pay overtime for a caretaker to be on the premises or have other expenses. If they do, it is up to you to decide whether your group can afford the charge.

So you've got permission - what next? It is important to agree with the owners about publicity. Some may want to publicise the watch, others may not. Respect those who want no publicity and warn the others that there should be none in advance. If a local newspaper mentions that your ghost watch is taking place on a particular night, the lager louts at the local pub will remember it at closing time and some lame brain will suggest to his pals that it would be great fun to go up the road and frighten the ghost watchers. As to publicity afterwards, the local press will be interested if you have some result. If you have good video or photographic material you may interest the national media.

Select a date for the event by reference to the availability of the location and the schedules of your group members. Saturday is a useful night, inasmuch as tired watchers can recover on Sunday before work on Monday. Set the hours of the watch by agreement with the owners. Ideally you should aim at the longest possible period, but the use of the premises may dictate starting and finishing times.

Find out as much as you can about what is alleged to happen on the the location and exactly where. If the place has any history, read it up. Whether you pass this knowledge on to your group is up to you. Some believe that it will predispose the watchers to see what they have been told about.

Make sure that your members know precisely how to get to the watch. Give them maps, bus numbers, nearest rail station etc. Confirm with them that they are taking part and let the owners know, as accurately as possible, how many people to expect. Draw up a list of what facilities you need from the owners and let them have it, in writing. If they can't accommodate some of your needs, discuss it with them and make other arrangements. A specimen list follows; it can be expanded if yours is a very complex operation or reduced for simpler watches:

1. Uninterrupted access to the experimental area between fixed times. Remember to include time at the beginning for setting up equipment, etc.

2. Mains power supply for video camera, tape recorder, etc. The location of this will depend on the length of your extension leads.

3. Watch area to accommodate the group. This needs to be a place which will allow all of you to sit in reasonable comfort with access to the experimental area. If you are using video monitoring it will need to be within the reach of your leads.

4. Access to toilets for your group.

5. Supply of tea/coffee/soft drinks during the watch. Make sure that it is clear whether you have to pay for these or not.

6. Breakfast for some or all watchers at the end of the session. Again - make sure who pays.

When these details have been clearly agreed with the owners, it is time to consider what equipment you need for the watch and whether you have it already or must buy, borrow or hire it. This involves thinking about what it is that you are trying to do.

Ghosts are seen, heard, felt or smelt. They may cause vibrations, temperature fluctuations, or electromagnetic disturbances. You need to set up the watch so that any of these effects can be detected by your watchers and if possible, measured and recorded by your equipment.

Do not be put off by movies that show paranormal researchers with pantechnicons full of sophisticated electronic equipment.

Ghosts are more often detected by people than by expensive arrays of computerised sensors. The basic instrument is a human being.

That said, some equipment is useful in attempts to detect, measure, or record paranormal phenomena, but the degree to which you invest in equipment is up to you. You may not believe that there have been benefits in the spread of the microchip, but the technology that gave civilisation the talking doormat, the singing Christmas card, musical underwear and the electronic parrot has also given ghost watchers access to inexpensive, portable devices that can assist in detecting, measuring and recording events. Here is a list that may help you which, again can be added to or shortened according to your needs.

1. Known human medium and/or experienced dowser - the best and least expensive detection equipment.

2. Video camera, recorder, monitor and extension leads long enough to reach mains point and carry signal to the watch room;

3. Still camera or cameras;

4. Tape recorder;

5. Movement detectors;

6. Compasses;

7. Thermometers;

8. Remote door bell unit or similar;

9. Note book, watch logbook, pens;

10. Batteries, tapes, video tapes, films for the above

As suggested, you can go into more or less detail than this list suggests. For example, some groups carry materials for sealing entries and exits to the experimental area and talcum powder or something similar to detect and record footprints. If you use these, remember to clean it all up in the morning. Some hang up paper party streamers to detect air currents, or mark out the experimental area with light coloured tapes so the position of anything seen can be estimated and it is easier to tell whether it is solid or transparent.

If you do not know a medium, psychic or dowser you can still try out the 'human detectability' factor of the premises. You and your group can perfectly well try your hand at receiving impressions from the area, or dowsing it. You may be surprised by the results.

While a video link is not a necessity, it makes keeping watch on an undisturbed area much easier, and if something occurs it might provide a record of it.

Where still cameras are concerned, a really useful piece of equipment is made by Konica. This is a 35 mm, auto focus, auto flash camera with a built in microphone. Devised, apparently, to take embarrassing pictures of noisy drunks at parties, the camera has a sophisticated sound analysis system that assesses the level of background noise in an area and ignores it. After that, any sound that rises above the background for a few seconds will trigger the camera to take a picture. There are three levels of sensitivity to which the microphone can be set and, in a silent area, it can be triggered by the rustle of paper. It costs about £70, but is, of course, a perfectly good ordinary camera when you are not embarrassing drunks or trying to photograph ghosts.

Tape recorders can be as simple as you like, but one with a voice operated (VOX) switch will save you the trouble of changing cassettes throughout the watch and listening to hours of blank tape afterwards. They cost about £30 or more from major electrical suppliers. It may also be worth adding the best microphone you can afford, and we suggest that you acquire a small broadcast standard mike (the kind they clip onto you in TV studios) for about £15. Used with even a simple, cheap recorder, it will improve the recording no end. If you use one, remember that they have a separate battery and see that it is in order.).

Movement detectors can be bought from electrical or security shops. You need not buy anything fancy. A small detector with a remote on/off setter can be bought for about £15.

Compasses are the easiest way to detect electromagnetic fluctuations. Buy them cheaply at camping shops. Thermometers can also be cheap and simple.

The remote door bell unit is not so that the ghost can ring it. Its use will be explained later, but they are also readily available quite cheaply. An alternative is an old fashioned doorbell with a long length of bell wire.

An instrument that you might like to add to the list is one made for gardeners. It has two programmable thermo sensors and a long wander lead. Each of the two sensors can be set to sound an alarm if the temperature drops or rises outside the preset range. One end can be in the watch area and the other in the experimental area. Unfortunately, these devices are relatively new and quite hard to find, but not expensive if you can locate one.

When you have assembled the equipment and arrived at the venue (in plenty of time) you should do a few things before setting up your equipment. If you have a medium in your group, allow them access to the experimental area, preferably on their own, and get them to note their impressions and any images they may have seen.

Next, if you have a dowser, let them work the area and mark out on a plan of the area any lines or areas that they consider significant. If you do not have a dowser, try it yourself or use volunteers. Dowsing rods can be very easily made from lengths of coat hanger wire bent into an L shape with sections of about three inches and twelve inches. They work better if you insert the short section into a piece of plastic tubing (cut a piece from an old ballpen) and hold the tube in your hand so that the longer section of wire points horizontally forward.

Walk the area slowly, with a rod in each hand. At some places the two rods may swing together. These are the significant spots. Try it - many people who have never done it before find that they are very good at it.

When any medium's or dowser's results have been noted you can set up the gear. First find the optimum place for your video camera, a spot that will give you the widest possible view of the allegedly affected areas. If you are dealing with a very big area, the results of dowsing and mediumship may help you to decide where something is most likely to occur, otherwise consult the owners.

With the video camera in place, put your monitor in the watch area, placing it so that it can easily be seen by as many people as possible. If you use a sound operated still camera, place it so the flash will not 'white out' the video image when it goes off. Compasses, if you have enough of them, can be placed around the watch area, and thermometers. Ideally, a compass and thermometer should be placed where they can be seen on the video monitor. Put your microphone reasonably near the 'target' area, set up your movement detector(s) - remembering NOT to switch them/it on, and lay out any tapes or streamers you want.

Finally, rig your remote doorbell with the sounder button in your watch area. When all the equipment is placed to your satisfaction, when the video monitor is producing a nice clear picture, the video tape is rolling and everything else is switched on, THEN you can set the movement detectors.

If you get that last bit wrong this is what will happen. Seconds after you set the detector it will shriek with alarm, probably because you are still blundering about in its beam. The shriek will set off the sound tape and the still camera, and the flash will blind the friend who's trying to adjust the video camera. We know this is true because we have a colour video of one of us doing it.

If you have got it all right, you can now retreat to the watch area, muster your group and begin the watch arrangements. The first important move is to remind them that it is very probable that nothing will happen all night.

Divide your party into teams of two or three persons and draw up a roster of 30 minute watch spells, each team taking turns at closely watching the video monitor. While they watch the monitor, they are responsible for making entries in the log. Ideally, you should be prepared with pages as follows:

Date:	Time:	Comment:	Signed:
23.2.97	1900	Team 1 commenced watch	
	1912	Yellow streamers moving gently	
	1915	Streamers now still	
	1930	Team 1 off watch	BR/FP
	1930	Team 2 on watch	
	1931	Still camera triggered by remote	
	1955	Red streamers moving gently	
	2000	Team 2 off watch	SQ/KT
	2030	Team 3 on watch	
	2001	Still camera triggered by remote	
	2011	Still camera triggered spontaneously (nothing visible on monitor)	
	2017	Red streamers now still	
	2030	Team 3 off watch	VC/JP

....and so on, relentlessly, all night long.

We have to tell you that a log so full of incident as the above would be a rarity. Most of the time nothing observable will happen and the log will show only the changes of watch teams.

Note the firing of the camera at each watch change. This is done by the remote door bell being sounded in the experimental area and simply provides a series of reference photos of the area. If the current watchers believe something is, or may be, happening in the experimental area, they can fire the camera on any occasion by sounding the bell.

Make sure that your watchers understand that anything at all that they see or think they see should be logged, as well as any strange feelings they have while on watch.

You will find that the group soon settle smoothly into the routine of changing watches and keeping the log. If there is a facility for displaying the time on the video monitor, use it as your official watch time for log purposes, then you will find it easier to compare log book entries with what is on the video tape. If not, you will need to ensure that each team has a watch and that they are all synchronised from the start.

As the night goes on, people will become drowsy, but you only require them to be alert during their half hour watches. Tell the group to bring with them whatever will help them through the night, whether it is lashings of tomato sandwiches, an improving book, a cuddly toy or whatever. Our own group seems to generate the most extraordinary discussions as the night wears on. Whether you forbid alcohol on the watch is up to you, but make sure that no one is likely to get drunk.

At the end of the watch, recover your equipment and tidy up after yourselves. Our group usually shares a breakfast before departing, purely because one house had cooks coming in early and offered to cook us one. Since then it has become a part of our operating pattern and makes a pleasant end to the night.

If you have followed the above advice you should now be able to mount a thoroughly professional ghost watch. If you require further advice, please write to us c/o the publishers of this book. If you have premises where our group can ghost watch, please also let us know.

Now that we have dealt with the theory, in the next few pages we shall describe three Watches in different kinds of buildings in the Midlands, so that you can see what happens in practice.

Haden Hill House, Oldbury

On a mild, sunny evening in early September, the group met at Haden Hill House in Sandwell. In our earlier book, *Midland Ghosts and Hauntings*, we included a brief history of the house and some comments on one of its most famous ghosts - the White Lady who has been seen drifting across the surface of one of the pools in the grounds.

The house lies between Halesowen Road and Barrs Road in Old Hill, surrounded by 60 acres of beautiful park. Designed and built in 1878 by George Alfred Haden Haden-Best, a Black Country millionaire, the Victorian house adjoins the remaining portion of the family's former Tudor mansion. In the 1920s the house was presented to the people of West Bromwich and is now administered by Sandwell Corporation, by whose courtesy we were the first group of ghost watchers permitted to remain in the house overnight.

Apart from the White Lady in the park, there are other reported hauntings at Haden Hill, including a lady in the dining room. To avoid spending an autumn night amidst the mists and dew of the grounds, we elected to go after the dining room manifestation.

The pool but no White Lady

The room is about 40 feet by 30, handsomely panelled, with a large bay window at one end looking south across the park. The only entrance is through double doors at the north-east corner of the room and on the west side is a large, black marble fireplace. On that evening the window was closed and shuttered on the inside with heavy wooden shutters.

Our watch area was established in the former housekeeper's room, only a few feet from the dining room. Before setting up our inanimate equipment, we let our medium and dowser examine the dining room in their own terms.

The medium reported that she had 'seen' a number of people: a man with a moustache and top hat, a woman in a green dress and a black boy in footman's livery. She had an impression of death or injury by fire in the room and reported feeling cold sensations in its north-west corner to the right of the entrance door. It should be said that the medium came from another area and knew nothing of the house or its alleged hauntings. Haden-Best was a man with a moustache, and presumably often wore a top hat. His wife appears in a portrait in the house in a pale turquoise dress. The Friends of Haden Hill society, some of whom stayed upstairs in the house that night, said that they had all the census details from the period when the house was occupied and that these did not show a black servant, nor did they know of any accident or injury by fire. Our medium was unaware that the figure that is supposed to haunt the dining room is that of a woman in a white dress.

Tony Serman, our dowser, detected a line of what he calls 'negative energy' running from the bay window, all along the west side of the room across the front of the fireplace. A second such line ran across the northern wall, the two lines crossing in the north-west corner to the right of the fireplace, the same corner where the medium had felt cold.

When our best detectors had finished we fell back upon technology. Justin Edgar, who ran the video equipment, placed his camera just inside the door, its view covering most of the room. In front of the window we put a sound operated camera on a table, pointing back towards the door, while a VOX tape recorder was stationed at the opposite end of the room, near the video camera. On the marble mantelpiece we put a motion detector. Compasses and thermometers were placed and paper streamers hung in the centre of the room. In the light of the medium's cold feelings, we took readings all over the room. There was no detectable cold area but a uniform temperature of 16 degrees Celsius.

The doors of the dining room were left open, watch teams set up and our watch began.

Several hours passed, during which nothing happened on screen and none of our detectors were activated. The tea and coffee supplied by the manager of the house, Clare Griffin, was steadily consumed and the groups conversations became more and more surreal. This is what happens on most ghost watches, and as tiredness sets in it can be difficult to maintain interest, but our watchers kept at it.

At about 0030 hrs Barrie went upstairs to the flat where a group of the Friends of Haden Hill were spending the night, and had a chat with them about what our group was doing. At 0100 he was on watch, but still nothing happened. The next watch took over and, at 0142 hrs everyone in the watch room saw a flash on the left hand side of the monitor.

We had been triggering our still camera at each change of watch, but that had been done at 0130. Twelve minutes later it had gone off spontaneously. Nothing unusual appeared on the monitor when the camera went off, but we assumed that a noise had occurred in the dining room.

Twice more during the watch, at just after 0300 and just before 0500 hrs the still camera fired spontaneously. Each time our watchers could see nothing on screen that could cause a noise. Speculation went on and on as to what could have triggered the camera.

After the 0400 hrs change of watch, we tried an experiment in 'distant influence'. Our whole party, some twenty people, gathered in the watch room and we decided to see if we could 'create' a noise in the dining room that would trigger the still camera. For five minutes all of us concentrated hard on creating such a noise, but no result showed.

The night wore on, the conversations became crazier and the sandwiches were all eaten, but at last the cooks came on shift and many of us enjoyed an excellent breakfast.

The last hour or so of the watch passed uneventfully. At 0800 the log was closed and we began recovering the equipment. We were doing this when one of the 'Friends' arrived from upstairs to enquire if some of our equipment had fallen in the night. His group had been wakened, just after 0400 by a loud bang from downstairs. We, of course, had all been awake and specifically listening for a noise at that time and we had not heard one.

When the cassette was taken out of the VOX recorder to be checked there were three strange bursts of noise on the tape, each relating to one of the times when the sound operated camera had fired. Our immediate impression was that it sounded like a heavy, pelting downpour of rain; others have described it as gravel being poured. It lasted for between 40 seconds and more than a minute and the recording was strong and clear, as though the noise was fairly close to the microphone.

We were nonplussed. There had been nothing in the dining room to make such a noise and we had heard no such sound from outside. The house's staff said they had never heard such a noise.

Pleased that we had some kind of result, however mystifying, we packed our gear, thanked Clare Griffin and crawled off to our beds.

A few days later the camera's film was processed. Every picture was identical. The three triggered by the mysterious noise showed nothing happening and nothing out of place in the dining room. A review of the twelve hours of video tape gave the same result.

The group had been warned at the outset that they might pass a sleepless night for nothing, but in fact we had a number of interesting facts to consider;

a) The images and impressions of our medium.

b) The location of the medium's 'cold spot' being the place where the dowser's two lines crossed.

c) The mysterious noise that woke the sleepers in the flat above at the time we were trying to create a noise in the dining room. Did their sleeping minds receive the impression of the sound we were trying to generate downstairs?

d) The triple rushing noise on the tape. We are having that electronically analysed, to determine whether the noise is natural or mechanical, though the problem will remain - that there was nothing of either kind there to make such a noise.

e) Members of the group reported feelings of unease, or sensations that something was peculiar, in other parts of the house, most particularly in the former laundry (now the cafeteria) and in the ladies' toilet.

There was one further incident, though whether it was evidence of paranormal activity we do not know. After talking to the Friend group upstairs, Barrie had gone on watch. It was twelve minutes after his tour ended that the still camera operated itself for the first time. Because of the time log displayed on the video monitor, he did not look at his watch during the rest of the night. Only when he got home did he discover that it had stopped at the time the camera went off. It was a good watch that had performed faultlessly for twelve years, but it has never worked since that night.

The watch at Haden Hill was successful inasmuch as it resulted in a small amount of information about an allegedly haunted site where no watch had been held before. We shall be happy to compare notes with anyone else who has information from Haden Hill or has experienced similar effects elsewhere.

Finally, we take this opportunity of thanking Sandwell Corporation and Clare Griffin and her staff for allowing the watch and for making us comfortable while we were at the house.

Walker's Bingo Hall, Wednesbury

Walsall Street, Wednesbury, is a short street just off the town centre. It most prominent building is Walker's Bingo Hall, a former cinema with a 60 foot tower which stands on the corner of the main road from Walsall.

Through the kindness of Wednesbury historian Ian Bott, we can tell you a little about the site. For many years (perhaps since the 17th century) a large family house stood on the site, but this was demolished before the Great War. It is possible that an early cinema of some kind was erected, but it is certain that in 1938 a new cinema opened there. It continued as a cinema into the late 1960s, when bingo took over, and the present building is substantially the same as in its cinema days.

Walkers gave us a tour of the building, from the basement where the original heating and ventilating equipment from the cinema still functions, to the former projection room at the top. Our guide was the maintenance engineer, a pragmatic gentleman who said that he was concerned with physical things and did not believe in ghosts. Nevertheless, he described how the computer keyboard that controls some of the equipment had misbehaved inexplicably on one occasion, one of its keys shooting from its place and bouncing round the office walls.

Staff told of a customer's little girl who had seen a figure in the ladies' toilet, and of a man seen in the basement. A former Manager had locked the hall one day and been surprised to see a figure on the stairs between the lobby and the balcony. He believed he was the only person in the building. The tall figure, apparently dressed in a long grey overcoat or cape, was going up towards the balcony, so the manager gave chase. Reaching the balcony, he was dumbfounded to find nobody there. In fact, he was so surprised that he retreated to his office and stayed locked in there until the evening staff came on.

We assembled at Walker's on a Saturday night after the customers had departed with their winnings. The start of our watch was delayed by the mysterious disappearance of two of our group, but at last we had to press on without them.

The stair landing, the ladies' and the basement were impossibly difficult to use as experimental areas, so we decided to locate on the balcony. Placing the video camera a little way from the left hand end, we established a watch area behind it from which we could observe the rest of the balcony and, if necessary, see into the main hall below. Our equipment was deployed, the watch teams allocated and the watch log opened.

It had turned six in the morning and no observable event had disturbed us, when one of the group drew attention to one of our compasses. Set with its needle pointing north at the beginning of the watch, the needle was now moving. We watched as the needles of both compasses (set on the outer edge of the balcony) edged away from north. After a few minutes they stabilised again, but this time both were pointing steadily about 5 or 6 degrees east of north.

Nothing else occurred. Neither video tape or camera film revealed anything, nor the sound tape, but those two compasses remained obstinately pointing to the wrong spot until we closed our watch. On Sunday morning we ate an enormous breakfast at the George Inn down the street, where the cellar is haunted by an old man in cap and muffler, and went home.

In the wake of that watch we tried to derive an explanation for the compass anomaly. Someone suggested that it was caused by ionization of the atmosphere as the sun rose. To test the theory, we took the same compasses and surrounded them with a battery of ionizers. The compass needles showed no movement whether the ionizers were switched on or off.

Our experiment eliminated ionization as an explanation, but not perhaps other effects of sunrise, though we would have thought that 5 or 6 degree compass errors caused by sunrise would make life at sea and in the air even more hazardous than it is already. We seem, however, to have given the lie to the oft quoted explanation of compass anomalies in the so called 'Bermuda Triangle' being caused by fluctuations in ionization.

Once again we had recorded a strange fact about haunted premises, but we are still seeking a solution. Shelagh Thomas, a long standing member of the group, believes that some source of power in the vicinity of the bingo hall was switched on at 0615 that morning and affected our compasses. She is currently trying to devise an experiment to test this.

What happened to our vanishing ghost watchers? Well, it seems that, having been told that Walker's was on Walsall Street, Wednesbury, 'a short commercial street that slopes down to the town centre', they located a 'Walsall Road' and deduced that they had been given a wrong name. They therefore ignored the fact that it wasn't a commercial street and did not slope into the town centre and did not have a dirty great bingo hall on it. After touring the area for an hour and a half, including a call at the police station, where they were told there was no bingo hall in town, they went home. Careful enquiry revealed that they had been in Darlaston, not Wednesbury.

We tell you this, eager ghost watchers, by way of underlining the fact that ignoring information and making a wrong assumption at an early stage can totally mislead you, whether you are trying to explain the paranormal or merely trying to find your way to Wednesbury.

Our group thanks Walkers, their manageress and staff for their facilities and hospitality, and the George Inn for a delicious ending to our Wednesbury watch.

Horsehay Engine Shed

You will find elsewhere in this book an account of the strange things seen, felt and heard by members of the Horsehay Steam Trust, a steam railway preservation society with premises on the southern edge of Telford. (The Haunted Engine) The Trust keeps and works on its engines in a Victorian engine shed, where most of these things take place.

Members of the Trust contacted us after reading *Midland Ghosts & Hauntings,* and on a bright, warm day in October 1995 we visited the shed. There we experienced for ourselves the sound of heavy boots walking along the ridge of the roof, a noise reported by members.

In early September 1996 the Trust held an open weekend of events and displays, and invited our group to hold a watch in the engine shed. Ten of us mustered there on a sunny but chilly evening.

The shed is essentially a large brick box, with an arched opening in its western end to allow engines to pass in and out. The arch can be closed by a steel drop shutter, and either side of it are bricked up smaller archways which were once doorways onto the internal platforms. The rails run about three quarters of the way into the shed with platforms on either side. Beyond the rails is an area with wooden doors at the east end. The north platform is narrow and gives access to a small office at the end of the rails. The south platform is wider and an outside door opens off it near the inner end.

We placed our video camera near the door on the south platform. One of the shed's ghosts had been seen and heard moving along that platform and leaving through the bricked up doorway at the end of the platform. We had a clear view along the platform. Another ghost is supposed to lurk around the Great Western 062 tank engine Number 5619, which we described under the story 'The Haunted Engine'. For our convenience that engine was drawn into the shed, with another one standing between it and the arched opening. Our camera's view covered the footplate entrance and the side of the allegedly haunted engine, as well as almost all of the south platform as far as the doorway.

Across the platform and extending its sensor area to the cab of the haunted loco, we set a movement alarm, with a sound recorder close by. When all equipment was placed, the watch teams were organised and we settled down in the little office on the north platform. Experienced members of the group soon got out their good books, bad magazines and sandwiches.

We fully expected a quiet, uneventful night, but soon discovered a difficulty. Although we had closed the big drop shutter at the west end, for about three hours after we began our watch we were regularly disturbed by people passing along the south platform from the side door to the shutter and vice versa. Fortunately we had upgraded our movement detector to one with an infrared remote setter, so it was not as much trouble as it might have been to keep resetting the alarm, but it did mean that our experimental area was constantly disturbed.

Once the last interloper had loped out, the hours passed without excitement and the yawns became wider and more frequent. Our last watch was to be from 0600 to 0630 hrs, leaving us time to evacuate before the trust's activities recommenced at 0700. It was 0614, according to the time log on the monitor, when the two people sitting nearest the screen both said 'What's that?' simultaneously. Both had seen movement on the monitor, as had two other viewers.

One had seen a shape move from between the two engines on the right of our picture, across the south platform to the left. Another had seen a shape start moving in the same area, but move away from the camera towards the bricked up archway. The other two had both seen a bright flash across the platform alongside the gap between the two engines.

We were cautious. It was near the end of our watch and tired eyes and minds can play tricks. Nevertheless, as soon as the watch ended, at 0630, we ran the video tape back and all of us watched carefully a replay of the minutes before 0615. Nothing the least bit unusual appeared on our black and white monitor.

Wondering whether we had recorded something or not, we breakfasted at a catering van. Bacon sarnies in the open air at sunrise have added zest. As we ate, the trust's personnel began to assemble, and Wendy Reynolds, chair of the Trust, asked if we had a result. We outlined what had happened in our last few minutes and she smiled. 'That's where I've seen him standing', she said.

That afternoon we played the last 30 minutes of video tape on a 30 inch colour screen. As soon as it started we noticed an anomaly. On our monitor in the watch room the picture was, as might be expected, more brightly lit in the foreground. We were not using additional lights - only the shed's ordinary lighting. In colour, while the foreground was adequately lit, the brightest area was further away, alongside the gap between the engines.

At that point it looked as though a single, bright light was creating a pool of brightness on the platform. As we watched, that brighter area began to shimmer or irridesce. Again, we were wary of tired eyes - we had then been without sleep for about thirty hours. However, another viewer, someone who had not been on the watch and did not know what we were looking for, asked 'Is it my eyes, or is that bright patch in the middle shimmering?' It was. We ran the tape again, and sure enough, the lighter patch does shimmer, not constantly but now and then, and it was doing so as 0614 appeared on the time log.

Is it an effect of the tape or the screen? We don't know. We must view that tape with other people on different recorders and screens to be sure. Is it an effect of the shed's lighting? Possibly. The trust have supplied us with a sketch plan of the lighting layout which reveals that only one of the pendant lamps over that platform was working that night, the one immediately over the area where movement was seen and where the bright patch appears on the video. That suggests that part of the effect is from the lighting contrast, but it does not explain why four people simultaneously witnessed movement at that point. We must also go through the sound tapes, though none of us heard anything unusual.

If what happened was paranormal, why didn't the tape record what people saw and why did four different people see three different things? Well, the failure of cameras to record what people definitely saw, or to record it differently, is one among the many mysteries of the paranormal. The only way to solve it is to keep on watching, recording and trying to make sense of the results.

We should add that after our watch a TV crew filmed in the shed. While they were doing so a member of the trust videoed them at work. At one point on that video a rhythmic clicking can be heard on the sound track. The trust referred the tape to us and we have viewed it and listened to it a number of times with Justin Edgar, the video producer who provides video facilities for our ghost watches. We believe that the noise is mechanical and close to the microphone. In fact, it sounds like something rapping lightly on the camcorder's body and might have been caused by a button, badge or something similar on the clothing of the person holding the camcorder.

The engine shed still held some surprises. A year after our first watch we were back, and this time we placed ourselves in a small shed beside the main building. We had with us no fewer than five mediums, all of whom believed that there was "something" in the shed. One said that the fireman alleged to haunt the engine had not come with it, but had died in an accident at Horsehay years ago and had relocated himself onto the Trust's engine.

Just before 11 pm Barrie walked through the shed to check that all was in order before we started the watch. Before leaving he took two photographs, one from immediately alongside engine 5718 and looking forward. After taking it he stepped one pace left and took another shot from a slightly different viewpoint.

The night wore on and the watchers logged many things they thought they had seen on the monitor screen, though few of them agreed with each other. Half an hour before the watch was due to end, Wendy Reynolds of the Steam Trust arrived with a camcorder to picture us in action. Minutes later there was an excited cry from the monitor watchers. A white mist was appearing, mostly under the roof of the engine's cab. As we watched the screen, Wendy took her camera into the shed at my request, and when she she came back she ran the tape again. The mist could be seen on her black and white monitor but was much less obvious later viewed in colour. Once again the shed was playing tricks, letting us see things that we could not, apparently, record.

Then Barrie had his photos printed. The first shot of the engine showed nothing unusual; the second, taken immediately afterwards and from almost the same viewpoint, revealed patches of white mist. They had not been visible to Barrie when he took the picture. They are not film or process faults. They lie within the frame of the picture on the negative, so they must derive from something that happened as that portion of film was exposed.

Barrie's photos

A mist that is invisible at 11 pm but appears on a photograph? A mist that is visible on monitor screens at 6.40 am but barely recordable. What is happening in the engine shed we do not know, but if the Trust continues to let us, we shall continue trying to find out.

Our thanks the committee and members of the Horsehay Steam Trust for the opportunity and for their hospitality and interest, most particularly Wendy Reynolds and Paul Noakes.